MW00476940

Gateway
to
Opportunity

HOW ONE PUBLIC
SCHOOL HELPED SHAPE
AN ENTIRE NATION

JAMES V. CAMMISA, JR.

Gateway to Opportunity

How One Public School Helped Shape an Entire Nation

Print ISBN: 978-1-66784-611-8
eBook ISBN: 978-1-66784-612-5

Dedicated to

The Boston Latin School Class of 1950.

*For its 224 graduates who were given the opportunity to realize the
American Dream.*

JAMES VINCENT CAMMISA

"Sonny" "Jim"   Harvard

"Unhappy, hope; happy, be cautious."

Entered Class VI from the Alexander Hamilton School
in 1944.
Fidelity Prize VI; John K. Richardson Prize III; Camera
Club I; German Club I; Highway Safety Club I; Literary
Club I; Modern History Club I; Register, Advertising Staff
I; 2nd Lieut. 9th Co. 2nd Regt.

Contents

Foreword

I MET JIM CAMMISA IN my office at Boston Latin School while he was working on this book and developing his concept of the relationship between education and The American Dream. Jim was certain that his Latin School education had been a major factor in his own success, and he had been researching Latin School history. He was also certain that the success of Latin School alumni from 1635 to the present was due in major part to the common rigorous educational experiences alumni had endured.

Jim examined the concept of the American Dream, a complex and always evolving optimistic aspiration for the future as interpreted in successive generations of Americans. The common thread from generation to generation he identified as education, and the exemplar of that common thread, the Boston Latin School, the oldest school in America, which has educated the children of Boston since 1635.

Latin School alumni have been cultural, political, religious, educational, and business leaders locally and nationally for nearly four centuries: philosophers, authors, composers, governors, senators, congressmen, judges, social agitators, ministers, priests, bishops, teachers, administrators, college presidents, entrepreneurs, managers, corporation presidents—Jim included anecdotes about many in his book to illustrate that preparation and readiness are essential to advancement.

It was my great pleasure to discuss elements of Jim's ideas and some of the Latin School history with him. He observed, and I have also seen, that many alumni when asked where they went to school reply "Boston Latin School" before mentioning a college, while most other college alumni name only the college.

Having worked at the school fifty-two years as teacher of English and later Assistant Head Master, I hope that some of what I had to say helped Jim in some small way in the writing of this excellent tribute to his alma mater.

Malcolm J. Flynn
Assistant Head Master Emeritus
Boston Latin School

Acknowledgements

THIS BOOK WOULD NOT BE possible without the unwavering support of Peter G. Kelly, class of 1983 and President of the Boston Latin School Association; as well as Malcolm Flynn who served the school for 52 years until his retirement as Assistant Head Master in 2016, and who selflessly donated his time poring over the content of this book. These distinguished gentlemen are true standard-bearers of the educational and character-building principles exemplified by the Boston Latin School.

Preface

THIS IS THE SECOND OF a sequence of books in the American Dream Book Series.

The first book dealt with the economic aspects of the American Dream—the belief in equal economic opportunity for all, a society where-upward mobility exists, and each generation can do better than the one before it. That book examined the stresses now placed on the Dream in the new twenty-first century free-market economy.

While conducting the research on the first book, it quickly became apparent to me that the foundation on which the American Dream is built is *education.* This is one of the main principles through which knowledge, skills, and values are acquired, and enable us to realize the Dream. What is most worrisome today, however, is the fact that deficiencies in the education of our young people may now be undermining the Dream. Every two years, the Organization for Economic Cooperation and Development (OECD) conducts world-wide studies of educational proficiency among fifteen-year-olds. Data comparing U.S. student performance to those of other nations is available for thirty-four countries. The data consistently show America's youth ranking in the bottom half in reading scores, science, and mathematics.

Educators in this country certainly understand and are addressing this problem. It's happening through new school accountability programs, higher teacher selection standards, and mandatory student testing. The purpose of this book, therefore, is not to rehash or present a debate on these issues. Leave that to professional educators. I am not one of them. What this book attempts to do is examine lessons from the past through the story of a public school that has been in existence for 380-plus years; what it did, and still does, for both its students and our country in fulfilling the American Dream.

I was fortunate enough to have attended that public school, the Boston Latin School, founded in 1635. It has a rigorous classical curriculum, and was a so-called gateway school, with virtually all its graduates going on to college.

Like myself in the 1950s, a large proportion of its students were first-generation Americans: the sons of Irish, Italian, Greek, and Jewish immigrants who came to our country at the turn of the twentieth century. From my graduating class, Harvard accepted forty-eight of us. Passing through this Latin School gateway gave us all an opportunity to succeed in life, to do better than our parents, and to lead fuller, richer lives. In thinking about this book, what became obvious to me is that the story of the Latin School would be a story of the American Dream.

Readers will quickly see that the book is a narrative history, written not by a professional historian, but a journalist. It tells a story—not in chronological detail, but rather a book that uses important events and iconic personalities from the school's rich history to showcase student aspiration, achievement, and fulfillment. The book is not written for academics or professional educators. Footnotes and citations were, therefore, not thought to be entirely necessary. Where significant, however, major sources are identified in the body of the text, or in the more detailed Appendix. It contains twelve exhibits, including a timeline chronology of the school's most historic milestones. There is also a complete bibliography.

The historical source material available for the book was quite extensive. The school's association of alumni was founded in 1844 and employs a full-time archivist. The Massachusetts Historical Society, the oldest in the nation, dates to 1792. These and other historical sources have been supplemented by interviews with alumni, as well as current and retired faculty members.

The book has been an exciting one to research and write. Although I personally spent six years as a young student at the Latin School, I have uncovered so much more about the school in working on this book. Age somehow gives one added perspective. The book has also given me the pleasure of renewing acquaintances with old schoolmates from the Class of 1950, to whom the book is dedicated.

James V. Cammisa, Jr.†
Bal Harbour, Florida

† Deceased, February 4, 2013

Prologue

THIS BOOK WAS WRITTEN BY my father, James Cammisa. In full transparency, it was edited and published posthumously—with some assistance from me, his middle son, Jeffrey, and two Boston Latin School associates. One morning in February of 2013, my father went to Office Depot to pick up copies of the book's manuscript. He was preparing to send these to his friends, Boston Latin School (BLS) associates, for their review and feedback. He collapsed in the check-out line from a heart attack and passed away a few days later.

I fondly remember my father's accumulation of yellow legal-sized notepads, newspaper clippings, and books with tattered tabs protruding from their pages. My siblings and I would often press him on why he held onto these papers and books. He would casually respond, "I'm saving them for my book." His first book, *The American Dream: How the Free-market Economy Is Eroding It and What We Can Do to Restore It* (ISBN 1463526115), was published over a decade ago. And alas, his second, *Gateway to Opportunity: How One Public School Helped Shape an Entire Nation,* delivers a remarkable perspective on his high school alma mater, the Boston Latin School—and covers the incredible journey of its alumni, many of whom were notable historic figures, in realizing the American Dream.

I have a host of excuses for not tending to this book sooner. Had I benefitted from the Latin School lessons and disciplines my dad was fortunate enough to receive, this might not have been the case. Nonetheless, I feel blessed to have completed this journey. It provided me an ongoing connection to my dad, whose insights and counsel I dearly miss. It is also my payback to him for the time he committed to helping me hone my own writing skills. I had decided to go into advertising after graduating college. One of the requirements for doing this was to build a portfolio of advertising spec work. My dad, having worked at Eastern Airlines in marketing for many years, and having taken part in the development of their *Wings of Man* campaign and

Walt Disney World partnership was the dream editor. He would regularly critique my work, and apply, I'm sure, many of the same rigorous teaching techniques practiced by the memorable Masters of the Latin School.

Having delved into the content of this book, I came to realize just how significant an impact his Latin School education had on him. It showed up in so many aspects of his life—ones that he modeled for his kids, and which I try to model for mine. One recurring joke in our family was his obsession for always being on time. This often meant arriving at airports hours before flight departures—which would often get delayed anyway. Or being the first to show up at parties and events. My dad attributed this pattern of behavior to the fact that his school masters would often lock the doors once class commenced at 7:45 a.m., leaving little hope for the tardy. But on a more serious note, right up until the end of his life, the Latin School experience was perhaps the most profound and beloved facet in his life—except for his wife, Barbara. What's just as remarkable is the incredible and unparalleled history of this iconic institution—and how many of its alumni were directly responsible for creating and fostering our nation. If those walls at the Latin School could only talk! But they can't, so this book will reveal to its readers a little of what transpired over the school's rich and unprecedented 388-year history.

Purchase, New York
Jeffrey Cammisa
February 2023

Introduction

THIS IS A STORY ABOUT one of the most iconic educational institutions in the U.S., one that has made unparalleled contributions to the fulfillment of the American Dream by so many of its graduates. The story begins as the seeds of a new nation were being sowed on our shores by a few hundred Englishmen and their families, in search of a better life. Over time, thousands more would arrive, settling in thirteen Atlantic coast colonies.

On July 4, 1776, these colonies joined together as a new nation. In the decades that followed, early settlers witnessed their nation grow and prosper. What began as just a dream, soon become a reality. America was indeed proving to be a land of opportunity for all, with an endless supply of resources, a venue where one could achieve a better, richer, and happier life, and a place where each generation could do better than the one before it.

This book traces the creation and evolution of the American Dream. It examines its origins in the Puritan settlements that were established in New England at the beginning of the seventeenth century. It also explores the foundation on which much of the American Dream was built. Unbeknown to many readers, the cornerstone of this foundation was set in motion in 1635, with the founding of the Boston Public Latin School (BLS or the Latin School).

BLS, or the Latin School, a Boston Public School, and the centerpiece of this book, is in fact the oldest school with a continuing existence in the nation today. Over the course of its more than 380-year history, the Latin School has stood out as an institution that has not only delivered a superb academic education, but more importantly, has instilled ideals and values that have propelled its graduates to transform the American Dream into a reality—or in today's lexicon, "living the dream."

The Latin School was patterned after English grammar schools that prepared young boys for university, with rigorous and disciplined classical curricula. Emphasis was placed on the Latin and Greek languages and cultures. In the historical chapters that follow, readers will be introduced to memorable classroom Masters, who not only instructed their students, but also instilled in them important lifelong virtues and values. Many of these Latin School Masters might have been lead characters in English novels and movie classics that portrayed traditional schoolmasters—stern, feared, yet highly respected.

It's also worth mentioning that during every period in U.S. history, the Latin School has produced a sizable number of prominent pupils who later helped shape and enrich the American Dream. Two Latin School alumni in particular, John Hancock and Samuel Adams, were deeply involved in the activities that fomented the Revolutionary War and were also later signers of the Declaration of Independence. The nineteenth century saw similar involvement of its alumni in important national events, including Charles Sumner and Wendell Phillips, leaders of the pre-Civil War abolitionist movement.

A large portion of this book is devoted to examining the educational philosophy and practices of the Latin School, and the role of faculty, curriculum, and standards of performance, and the school's role in forging important virtues and character traits in its students.

In interviews with fellow alumni in writing this book, responses consistently homed in on the virtues and values students acquired while at the school—ones that propelled graduates to significance in later life. Although the classroom lectures may be long forgotten, the lessons learned, and character developed will never fade. These recollections were always described fondly in vivid detail by alumni, even though their Latin School experience may have occurred many years ago.

Although the Latin School history is the primary subject of this book, it is the author's hope that readers will come away with a broader understanding and appreciation of what educational excellence can contribute to our nation's preeminence, and fulfillment of the American Dream. What follows is a hall pass to history.

CHAPTER I

Building Blocks of the American Dream

You see things; and you say "Why?"
But I dream things that never were; and I say, "Why not?"

—GEORGE BERNARD SHAW

THE PHRASE AMERICAN DREAM WAS not coined by politicians or pundits. Nor was it intended to be a bumper sticker or rallying cry. Rather, it was meant to signify so much more. It was designed to serve as a set of principles upon which all people could flourish. The phrase itself, the American Dream, is credited to an American colonial historian, James Truslow Adams, who in 1931, published a book entitled *The Epic of America*. His work, ironically written during the Great Depression, dealt with the historical events and issues that he believed would have significant bearing on shaping the American character. Adams, who shared no relation to any U.S. presidents, envisioned a dream that consisted not of material possessions, but rather moral elements. In his book, Adams defined the American Dream as follows:

> The American Dream is that dream of a land in which life should be better and richer and fuller for every man, with opportunity for each

according to his ability or achievement ... It is not a dream of motor cars and high wages merely, but a dream of social order in which each man and each woman shall be able to attain to the fullest stature of which they are innately capable, and to be recognized by others for what they are, regardless of the fortuitous circumstances of birth or position.

Adams's work was the focus of many other scholars over the decades. In one well-researched book, *The American Dream: A Short History of an Idea that Shaped a Nation,* Jim Cullen, a writer, and professor of American civilization, explored the multi-faceted dimensions of the Dream. His analysis included the notions of equality and upward mobility and provided a blueprint for forging the American character. Scholars agree that the Dream should not be interpreted as a political, economic, or social doctrine. Rather it should be embraced as a cultural ideal, or aspiration—much like any national ethos or credo, a common set of ideals, attitudes, values, and beliefs which cultural historians agree have influenced the way Americans see themselves and their nation. The Dream has had other connotations as well. Included among these was a sense of possibility, high expectations, and personal fulfillment. It embraced the notion that working hard and doing right would enable anyone to succeed in the land of opportunity. It echoed a "can-do" attitude, characterized by optimism, and hope about a brighter future. Central to this notion was the idea that our children could do even better than we ever could do for ourselves by becoming better educated and taking advantage of living in an upwardly mobile society. Yes, it's true, our country was blessed with bountiful national opportunities and resources, but it would take the American work ethic, often hard labor and sweat equity, to truly reap its rewards.

Over the years, scholars have used a series of descriptive phrases that lend greater clarity to what the American Dream means, including concepts like freedom, justice, work, education, excellence, frugality, family, and community, to name just a few. Several Calvinist values were also attributed by many scholars: self-reliance, enterprise, hard work, austerity, and one's obligation to community. Although these may smack of religious tenets, they are believed to also apply to America's secular culture, even today.

Although the American Dream has become common vernacular, its origins date far back, before it was ever called anything, but rather was a way of life.

PURITAN IDEALS

The real birth of the American Dream occurred in 1630 alongside John Winthrop's Massachusetts Bay Company. An English barrister and religious reformer, Winthrop financed a fleet of eleven ships with 700 individuals sailing from England in 1630, ten years following the landing by the Pilgrims at Plymouth Rock. Winthrop's settlements were established along the shores of what is now known as Boston Harbor. He would serve as the company's leader for most of the next twenty years.

The new settlers were not explorers, adventurers, or traders. Rather, they were entire families who chose to separate from the Church of England and form a holy commonwealth of their own. They were in search of a better life in a new land, and thus was born the American Dream.

Hard work would be necessary for this dream to be realized. Geography was not in the Puritans' favor. Unlike the Jamestown settlement of Virginia, which was the first permanent English settlement in the New World, and which benefited from warm climate and fertile soil, New England soil was of glacial origin and short summers made raising crops difficult. The settlers would have to look to the forests, rivers, and streams as resources from which they could build their colonial economy. Fishing, hunting, and shipbuilding, therefore, quickly became important local industries. Individual entrepreneurs made up a large portion of the workforce—tanners, blacksmiths, masons, wheelwrights, glaziers, and millers. Underlying these occupations was the presence of a strong work ethic. In later years, scholars would connect this ethos back to a building block of the American Dream. The Puritans believed that self-discipline and hard work was their calling—not for a better life in the hereafter, but for here on Earth today.

The Puritans also believed that their new society would be a model for others to follow. Prior to their landing while aboard John Winthrop's flagship, *The Arbella,* he gave his famous "City Upon a Hill" sermon that proclaimed, "For we must consider that we shall be as a city upon a hill with the eyes of all people upon us."

It may come as some surprise, but according to many scholars, it was the religious teachings practiced by the Puritans that contributed most to their ability to build a successful new world society. The Puritans believed in separation of church and state. This, as we know, is one of the foundations of our democracy. The Puritans also believed in egalitarianism, or social equality, which permitted parishioners to participate in religious ceremonies and church matters. The congregation was essential and in striking contrast to the top-down hierarchal structure of the then-prevailing Protestant and Catholic churches they left behind in Europe. The congregation would later become the model for the well-known New England town meeting, where every citizen enjoyed freedom of speech, later cited by Franklin Roosevelt as one of America's Four Freedoms.

Over the years, there has been a lot of criticism of the Puritans and their beliefs. Yes, in some respects, they have been characterized as fanatical, uncompromising, and stubborn. The Salem Witch Trials in 1692 are cited as an example of their fanaticism. Despite this criticism, what they did leave their descendants was a set of beliefs, values, and standards that were the beginnings of the American Dream.

THE DECLARATION OF INDEPENDENCE

As historians have examined and re-examined every word in the Declaration of Independence, what was, and continues to this day, to be at the center of debate is the phrase, "that all men are created equal"; created equal, that is, amongst white men. Equality for women and Blacks continued to be on hold for many more generations, with serious moves for equal rights not beginning until 1848, when social activist Elizabeth Cady Stanton organized the first important women's conference in Seneca Falls, New York. There, this group drafted a Declaration of Sentiments, which was closely patterned after the Declaration of Independence. It outlined demands for equal rights in marriage, education, religion, employment, and public life. Following this ambitious start, the movement continued, only slowly. It wasn't until 1920, with the ratification of the nineteenth amendment to the Constitution, that women received the right to vote—144 years after the Declaration of Independence was signed.

For African Americans, the road to equality would also be a long, difficult one, with the first of many existing barriers to equality not removed until eighty-six years after the Declaration of Independence was signed. The Emancipation Proclamation, in a series of two executive orders, was issued in 1862 and 1863, followed by the thirteenth amendment that banned slavery completely; and finally, the fifteenth amendment in 1870. The latter amendment declared that "the rights of citizens to vote could not be denied on account of race, color, or previous conditions of servitude."

Equality for African Americans would still take a good deal longer, and not gain real momentum until the Supreme Court's 1954 *Brown vs. the Board of Education* ruling ending school segregation. The Civil Rights movement, as we know it today, really began after a seat in the white section of a Montgomery, Alabama bus was denied to Rosa Parks. Martin Luther King, Jr. was now front and center, and his enormous influence would be felt until his death in 1968 and is still felt to this day. King was able to witness the passage of the *Civil Rights Act* in 1964, banning discrimination in employment practices and accommodations. Following that, the *Voting Rights Act* outlawed a variety of discriminatory voting practices.

Despite the progress made during the 1960s, African Americans had much further to go before they could begin to share in the American Dream. In one of history's most memorable speeches, Martin Luther King,

Jr. expressed his hopes for the future. Standing at the foot of the Lincoln Memorial in Washington on August 28, 1963, before a crowd of 250,000 in attendance that day, King delivered his famous "I Have a Dream" speech in which he said the following:

> In spite of the difficulties and frustrations of the moment, I still have a dream. It is a dream deeply rooted in the American Dream ... that one day this nation will rise up and live out the true meaning of its creed: "We hold these truths to be self-evident: that all men are created equal."

Although the Declaration of Independence was clearly flawed in not representing the rights and freedoms of African Americans, it was a different time, and perhaps a precursor to one of the most important Dream building blocks that echoed in King's moving words.

THE RISE OF THE COMMON MAN

On the fiftieth anniversary of the signing of the Declaration of Independence, a remarkable and historical coincidence occurred—two of the Declaration's most prominent signers passed away on the exact same date. Thomas Jefferson passed away at his home in Virginia. John Adams at his home in Massachusetts.

The deaths of our Founding Fathers marked the end of an era, and the beginning of another. The country was moving from an agricultural society, supported by small freeholder farms, to a commercial and industrial one, where an increasing proportion of the population were wage-earners. Land interests of the earlier era were represented in government by aristocrats. All six presidents, four from Virginia, and two from Massachusetts, had wealth-related or aristocratic backgrounds.

As with most periods of historical change, the circumstances of the time brought forth new and different political leaders. Andrew Jackson would come forth as that leader in 1829, championing the rights of the common man. Born to Irish immigrants in a backwoods Tennessee town, he would distinguish himself in military uniform as a courageous Native American fighter and foe of British tyranny. Nicknamed "Old Hickory" for his reported toughness, Jackson fought in both the Revolutionary War and the War of 1812. His overwhelming victory at the Battle of New Orleans in 1815 was the last battle of the War of 1812 and is considered to be the most dramatic and a key milestone in Jackson's life.

Jackson's military accomplishments, and some of the myths surrounding them, were factors that got him elected to the presidency in 1829. His election was heralded as a victory for the common man—the farmers and laborers who made up America at the time. For the first time in history, these groups would also be invited to his presidential inauguration. They came in droves, and reportedly the White House and its lawn were covered in mounds of debris left by the celebrants. Yes, a common, self-made man such as Jackson could succeed in America, and one day become president. Let the celebration begin!

Historian Arthur M. Schlesinger, Jr., in his Pulitzer Prize-winning book *The Age of Jackson*, called out the historical significance of the Jackson administration in terms of its progressive cultural, social, and economic aspects. While in office, Jackson supported causes that were important to ordinary citizens. His vice president and successor, Martin Van Buren, said that Jackson believed, "To labor for the good of the masses was a special mission assigned to him by his Creator." Jackson took strong positions against the bankers and was instrumental in broadening voting rights to any white male citizen. Previously, only property owners could vote. During his term and thereafter, judges would be elected by the people rather than appointed. The symbolism associated with a hardscrabble common man reaching the highest office in the land helped to solidify the American Dream.

At the time Jackson left office in 1837, a twenty-eight-year-old lawyer from Springfield, Illinois was becoming the century's most iconic common man—none other than Abraham Lincoln. Born in a one-room log cabin, Lincoln was self-educated, admitting that he had no more than eighteen months of formal schooling. The most notable thing about Lincoln, in the context of the American Dream, was that he was the quintessential self-made man—an American icon who embodied values inherent in the Dream.

The notion of the common man and its archetypal role in building the Dream would be a recurring theme throughout U.S. history. Reflexively we can recite individuals who helped to perpetuate and enrich the Dream: Adams, Franklin, Revere, Hamilton, Hancock, Emerson, and the list goes on and on. These iconic figures were the torchbearers of this ideal, and they all made an indelible mark on history. But the white elephant in the room cannot be ignored. It's reasonable for one to wonder, what about all the deep social, geographic, and economic rifts that exist today in our country? If the American Dream can be summed up as a promise of prosperity and mobility for all, including the common man, isn't the American Dream unequivocally at risk—or worse, a fallacy?

Our role as citizens, whether directly or indirectly through our actions, is to preserve the American Dream's tenets and expand its reach—as it always was intended to be. Because the Dream has contributed so much to our well-being and the nation's prominence, it must not erode, be weaponized, or used as a prop for political gain. It must be preserved as it was originally conceived, with the goal of providing future generations of Americans a better life. Hopefully, by having greater context around how the Dream came to be and meeting those individuals who helped create and nurture it, we will have taken an important step toward keeping it alive.

Remarkably, at every significant point in U.S. history, it can be said that the Boston Latin School is the geolocation for the American Dream. The school has been responsible for a sizable number of prominent pupils, most of whom went on in life to help shape the Dream—from signers of the Declaration of Independence to eminent political leaders; from noted authors to famous musical composers; from Fortune 500 business leaders to educators and mentors. All are not only alumni of this iconic educational institution, but also have been instilled with the values that have kept the American Dream not just a dream, but a reality.

CHAPTER II:

Education and the American Dream

Education, beyond all other devices of human origin is the great equalizer of the condition of men, the balance-wheel of social machinery.

—HORACE MANN

ONE OF THE MOST IMPORTANT elements of the American Dream is equality of opportunity. This means, regardless of one's background, everybody has the unalienable right to pursue the dream of a better, more prosperous, and happier life. To achieve these ends, education must serve as gateway through which the doors of opportunity open.

The early settlers, and generations that followed them, used education as an essential part of achieving the Dream. Education offers every individual the knowledge and skills needed to pursue and fulfill one's God-given potential. Education instills the values and virtues needed in a well-ordered society. It prepares us to become responsible citizens, helping us to grasp political issues, and choose our leaders wisely. The Founding Fathers knew that educated leaders would be needed to follow in their footsteps, and that an educated citizenry was necessary to make their new democracy work. As early as 1779, Thomas Jefferson proposed a three-tier plan for public education in Virginia, calling for elementary schools for young children, grammar schools for more advanced students, and college for the more talented. With the latter in mind, Jefferson was influential in reforming the curriculum and governance of William and Mary College.

Education also accomplished another important national objective, that of aiding in the assimilation of immigrants into the American society, providing the sons and daughters of these immigrants a roadmap for realizing the Dream. An early twentieth-century educator, Ellwood Cubberley, saw this as the central role of education:

> To assimilate and amalgamate [people] as part of our American race, and to implant in their children ... the Anglo-Saxon conception of rightness, law and order, and to awaken in them a reverence for our democratic institutions.

During the peak years of immigration between 1870 and 1920, there were about 26 million new arrivals to the U.S. Almost 90 percent came from non-Anglo countries, the bulk of whom came from Eastern and Southern Europe. With the children of immigrants enrolled in public schools, they would learn our language, study our history, and gain an understanding of the ideals and values that would enable them, like those before them, to advance in our society.

Clearly, it was education's goal to do much more than simply impart knowledge or teach students skills. It also needed to impart virtues and build character in students. Benjamin Franklin recognized many of these dimensions of education:

> Nothing can more effectually contribute to the cultivation and improvement of a country, the wisdom, riches, and strength, virtue and piety, the welfare and happiness of a people, than a proper education of youth, by forming their manners, imbuing their tender minds with principles of rectitude and morality, [and] instructing them in ... all useful branches of liberal arts and science.

Noted philosopher and educator John Dewey also saw education in a similar light: "To give one command of himself, to train him so he will have the full and ready use of all his capacities."

For our society to truly reap education's rewards, prominent thinkers believed schooling should not be limited to the few, but rather more broadly available to everyone: public education that was free to all. New England was on the forefront of establishing a public education system in colonial America. Early settlers, many of whom were artisans and tradesmen, were quite literate, and understood the value and importance of learning and education.

Puritan theology had the strongest influence in driving education. The Puritans held strong to the belief that knowledge of the Scriptures was essential, even mandatory, as it required reading and understanding Biblical lessons.

Prior to the establishment of public schools, home served as the learning center. Fathers bore the responsibility of teaching their sons, particularly instilling the skills needed to follow father's footsteps. Men were also responsible for teaching apprentices or indentured servants living in their household. On the other side of the aisle, mothers were expected to teach their daughters virtues and homemaking skills that would prepare them for marriage.

Formal town-supported schools got their start in 1635, with none other than the Boston Public Latin School, which at the time, was called a grammar school. Over the next 125 years in colonial America, public education would expand, with other colonies mirroring the New England model, creating elementary and grammar schools. After Independence, New England continued as the pacesetter in public secondary education. In 1821, the Boston School Committee, a governing body of the Boston Public Schools, authorized the opening of the first public high school, the Boston English Classical High School, later shortened to Boston English High School. This school was created to educate working-class schoolboys in preparation for business, mechanics, shopkeeping, and trades—unlike the Boston Latin School that prepared students for college, professions, ministry, and scholarly or political pursuits. The courses offered at the Boston English School were seen as practical ones, what would be referred to as a trade or tech school today, and prepared graduates for the growing number of skilled jobs needed in the burgeoning New England economy.

One of the oldest school football rivalries in the country is that between the Boston Latin School, the oldest public school in the nation, and the Boston English High School, the oldest high school. Every Thanksgiving Day, for more than 130 years, the two football teams have faced one another in a season-ending, and often climactic game at Harvard Stadium, the site of the nation's oldest university.

As the nineteenth century got underway, the benefits associated with public education were widely accepted. Institutions became known as "common schools." The term was one used by Horace Mann, who was a New Englander appointed as the first Massachusetts state education secretary in 1835. An energetic and hard-working official, Mann rode from town to town on horseback, inspecting schools and making recommendations for improvement. He too saw the importance of common schools to serve as an equalizer in our society: "It is a free school-system, it has no distinction of rich and poor; it throws open its doors and spreads the table of its bounty for all the children of the state."

Through the efforts of Horace Mann, in 1852 Massachusetts became the first state to pass compulsory school attendance, or truancy laws. Mann continually pushed the leveling effect that public schools would have, and insisted that merit should be able to rise, regardless of one's background. His opinions truly reflected the linkage between education and the American Dream's virtues of self-improvement and personal achievement.

As the years passed, state and local commitments to compulsory public education continued to increase. Common elementary schools were the starting point for this trend, followed by public secondary schools, including what is known as high school today.

CHAPTER III

The Colonial Period Begins

"In every phenomenon, the beginning remains always the most notable moment."

—THOMAS CARLYLE

THE STORY OF THE BOSTON Latin School begins in the spring of 1635. It started on the Shawmut Peninsula, renamed Boston a few years earlier by Governor John Winthrop. There were fewer than a thousand residents of this new town, the strongest of whom had survived a third New England winter. Two hundred had died during the first winter. But as each winter passed, the settlers increasingly adjusted to their new and challenging environment. They were now ready to move forward in building the new "City Upon a Hill." Winthrop had already set in motion this endeavor with the inspirational sermon he delivered aboard the *Arbella* during its voyage to America. A few years after the settler's arrival, there is the record of a resolution signed by several of the Puritan leaders with a focus, yes, on education. It stated that:

> After God has carried us safely to New England, and we had builded
> our houses, provided necessaries for our livelihood, reared convenient
> places for God's worship, and settled the city government; one of the

next things we longed for and looked after was to advance learning and perpetuate it to posterity.

The Puritan settlers recognized learning and education as a cornerstone for the prosperity of individuals and their communities. The motivation was primarily a religious one, with literacy deemed to be a prerequisite to reading and understanding the scriptures. But the settlers also saw that only through education would one be able to grasp the knowledge necessary for state leadership. They not only wanted to advance learning, but to perpetuate it as well. The actual word *perpetuate* appears in several early Puritan documents, reflecting a desire to keep strong religious beliefs alive for future generations.

Though there are no official records to indicate the types of schools that colony leaders thought necessary to accomplish their goals, there were probably discussions on the merits of establishing elementary schools for younger children versus those for more advanced and older ones. If this debate took place, we might predict the outcome based on the needs of the times: schools for elementary age children could wait, as young children were being educated in the home by their parents. They were learning to read, write, and cipher. It was not until 1647 that early public-school education was mandated—a law requiring that once a town reached fifty households, it would have to have a schoolteacher. Those with 100 or more households would require a grammar school as well.

Schools for older children were to win this theoretical debate, with the founding of the Boston Latin School on April 23, 1635—the only college preparatory grammar school. The school's founding was recorded with this notice, "At a general meeting upon public notice, it was generally agreed upon that our brother, Philemon Pormort shall be entreated to become schoolmaster for the teaching and nurturing of children with us." Thus, the cornerstone of the foundation of the American Dream was put in place with the opening of the nation's first free and public school.

Phillips Brooks, a notable Latin School alumnus and nineteenth-century Episcopal Bishop of Massachusetts, described the importance of the school's open and public enrollment in the following way:

> Side by side on its humble benches sat the son of the governor and the son of the fisherman, each free to take the best that he could grasp. The highest learning was declared at once to be no privilege of an aristocratic class, but the portion of any boy in town who had the soul to desire it and the brain to appropriate it.

The decision to establish a college preparatory school such as the Latin School is understandable. Virtually all Puritan leaders were university educated. Most had also been educated themselves at English grammar schools, after which the Boston Latin School was patterned. They all understood the value of higher education, and the necessity to lay the foundation for a university pathway, if they wanted to see their Puritan ideals last beyond their own lifetime. The clock was ticking.

THE SCHOOL'S FOUNDING FATHERS

Those who study our nation's history most likely have always had an interest in understanding individuals who were founders of major institutions—company founders, those who founded major libraries, museums, and educational institutions. Over the course of history, there are certain traits that successful founders of companies or larger institutions share. A popular business magazine once characterized these founders as having a healthy obsession with solving problems. That's the stuff that drives most founders to take giant leaps of faith when starting their own business. Finding people who share in that obsession is critical to building a strong founding team. And that's exactly what brought founders of the Latin School together to create the first and most sustainable public education institution our country has ever known.

From a research perspective, identifying the founders of the Boston Latin School is no small task. Due to the limited availability of public records in the early days of the Boston settlement, it is difficult to exactly pinpoint people, places, and events. What can be done, however, is piece together records that do exist, and connect the dots with the activities and historical events happening during that time. It's essential to understand who these founders were to lend insight into the formation of this iconic institution. With this in mind, it appears that there were three groups of individuals in the Boston community who can be considered the school's true founding fathers.

The first group consisted of magistrates who held offices both before and during the founding years. There were three individuals within this group: John Winthrop, Henry Vane, and Thomas Dudley. A second group provided the initial funding for the school. There is a record stating that, "Richer inhabitants, forty-five in number, made generous voluntary contributions of between forty and fifty pounds towards the maintenance of a free schoolmaster." This amount would be equivalent to roughly $9,300 today. And finally, the third group of founding fathers consisted of a single individual, the Reverend John Cotton, who many believe was the most influential of all the founders—due to his work in gathering support for the school, shaping its curriculum, and overseeing its instructional methods.

John Winthrop

The Massachusetts Bay Company charter bears the name of John Winthrop. This was a joint stock trading venture that was chartered by the English crown and used to fund the colonization of New England. Winthrop was one of twelve who signed the charter in 1629, only six years prior to the Latin School being founded. A year later his fleet of ships arrived at Salem, and then sailed a few miles south to establish the new town of Boston. Over a twenty-year period, Winthrop was elected governor twelve times. John Winthrop is remembered as a gentleman, bookish, and conscientious. His education began at an English grammar school, Bury St. Edmunds, an experience that would be invaluable to him later in establishing a Latin grammar school here in the new colony. From grammar school, he went on to Trinity College at Cambridge. He then practiced law in London and was admitted to the prestigious Gray's Inn at the age of twenty-six. For most of his years, Winthrop kept a diary. Scholars who have studied it indicate that he had strong beliefs about the values of higher education and the preparatory paths that were necessary for individual advancement. At the time of the Latin School's founding, he was deputy governor of the colony.

Henry Vane

A late arrival to the Colony, Henry Vane was a wealthy twenty-two-year-old English magistrate who came to Boston in October of the year that the Latin School was founded. He served as governor in 1636-1637, the start-up years for the school. His name is also listed in the group of forty-five people who provided the initial school funding. Highly respected by his colleagues, he was considered an important supporter of the school and its goals during its formative years.

Thomas Dudley

Among those in the colonial government, Thomas Dudley is perhaps considered another important but supporting player. Working with John Winthrop, he was one of the organizers in England of the Massachusetts Bay Company and sailed to America with Winthrop. Dudley was the governor from 1634-1635, during which time plans for the Latin School were being finalized. He later served in that office for three additional terms. Reflecting his strong beliefs in the importance of education, he was also on a committee formed to establish Harvard College. Later, as governor, he signed the school's charter, and was an Overseer. In 1935, a non-resident center at the college was opened and named in his honor. It was, and still is, a gathering place for the many less-affluent Latin School boys who went on to Harvard, and each day commuted from their homes to the college.

John Cotton

The Massachusetts Bay Colony was fortunate to have among its leaders one of the most prominent clergymen in seventeenth-century England. His grandson, Cotton Mather, remembered John Cotton as "a walking library, who believed that twelve hours should make a scholar's day." Cotton was born in 1584, grew up in Derbyshire, England, and attended one of the country's oldest grammar schools in preparation for his university studies.

A brilliant student, he earned degrees from both Trinity and Emmanuel College at Cambridge. At the latter, he also served on the faculty. At the age of twenty-seven, as a clergyman, he was appointed Vicar at St. Botolph's in Boston, Lincolnshire, where he served for twenty years. Active in community affairs, each week he gave his famous inspirational Thursday lectures, which every schoolboy was required to attend. Many of those boys were from the Free Grammar School in the town, a school that would later be a model for New England's Boston Latin School. In his long tenure as an active and interested community leader, he would have had a deep involvement with the Free Grammar School and would later draw on this experience in helping to establish and shape the character of Boston Latin School.

Cotton's relationship with the Massachusetts Bay Company began in 1630, when John Winthrop invited him to Southampton to give the farewell sermon to passengers bound for America aboard the *Arbella*. Three years later, he himself would leave England. His arrival in Boston was enthusiastically welcomed, as most of the colonial leaders knew of him previously, and of his reputation as both a scholar and eloquent preacher. It is probably no coincidence that eighteen months after his arrival, a new grammar school, patterned after the one in Boston, Lincolnshire, would be opened. There are no records showing specifically what he did to help found the school, but we do know that whenever there was a record dealing with education in the colony, his name was usually included.

Long-time Latin School Master Philip Marson, who upon retirement in the 1960s wrote three books on the Latin School, believed that Cotton's strongest influence was in the development of the Latin School curriculum, and its high standards of performance. Marson points out that Cotton also saw the necessity of closely linking together grammar school and college curricula—in this case, a classical curriculum that included the study of Latin and Greek. As final evidence of a John Cotton-Latin School connection, upon his death, Cotton left half of his estate to the school.

Records indicate that all the Latin School founders knew each other well and worked closely with one another. They all had Boston, Lincolnshire roots. Winthrop and Dudley had jointly organized the Massachusetts Bay Company and arrived together on the *Arbella*. Winthrop, Vane, and Dudley all rotated in positions as colonial magistrates—sometimes as governor, or deputy governors, or in other government advisory roles. Records also indicate that Cotton and Vane shared lodgings. These Latin School founders were as much founding brothers as they were founding fathers.

THE ENGLISH GRAMMAR SCHOOL

The basic educational philosophy, curriculum, and instructional methods that were established for the Latin School at its founding were all modelled after those of English grammar schools. High standards of excellence, requiring intensive study habits, rigorous mental conditioning, and arbitrary rules of discipline would be employed. Study of Latin and Greek would be the foundation of a classical liberal arts education, in which students would be taught to translate, understand, and be able to discuss the works of ancient scholars.

Early educators often referred to the Latin phrase *via trium,* which means three ways, to describe what a classical education encompasses: grammar, logic, and rhetoric. Grammar was seen as the study of language, its usage, and rules of syntax; logic related to interpretation, reasoning, and synthesis; and rhetoric, not surprisingly, the art of verbal and written communication.

John Winthrop's biographer, Francis J. Bremmer, offers insights into the grammar school Winthrop was believed to have attended in England, known as Bury St. Edmunds. It probably was like other English grammar schools of the seventeenth century. In its statutes, written in 1586, were some of the following governing principles:

- No scholar was to be admitted unless he can read and write competently.

- No scholar shall continue in the school above five years, or six at most.

- Students are to be divided into groups, with the schoolmaster teaching the lower forms, the Head Master, the other students.

- No scholar was to appear in school unkempt.

- Order was to be maintained, with severe punishment inflicted for noise, pilfering, lies, swearing, or speaking words of ribaldry.

English grammar school pupils were usually seven to fourteen years of age, with those ten to fourteen seen as the advanced group. The school year usually ran forty to forty-four weeks, with a school day lasting from six in the morning until five in the evening during the summer months; and seven in the morning until four in the evening, during the winter months. There would be a two-hour break at midday. Classes were conducted five days a week, which included a half-day for a mandatory Thursday-town lecture.

In addition to teaching academic subjects to prepare students for college, the grammar schools saw their role as instilling meaningful values, ideals, and disciplines into their pupils—character traits that would forge them into stronger individuals and prepare them to become more valuable members of their communities.

THE LATIN SCHOOL-HARVARD CONNECTION

For more than 380 years, there has been a close and important connection between the Boston Latin School and Harvard College. The bond began with the founding of the college in September 1636, just thirteen months after the Latin School opened its doors. The same individuals who were the Latin School's founding fathers were instrumental in the founding of Harvard. When, in 1636, the Massachusetts General Court authorized the establishment of the college with a grant of £400, Messrs. Winthrop, Vane, and Dudley, were all members of that legislative body. In 1637, when the general court followed up with the appointment of a twelve-man committee, "for a college at Newtown" (later renamed Cambridge), Winthrop, Dudley, and Reverend

John Cotton were appointed to the committee. Henry Vane, the fourth of the Latin School founders, had returned to England, and therefore was no longer associated with the group. The common bond among these men was seeing higher education as a continuum, with the grammar school preparing and moving young boys on to a college education—the educational model they all had experienced previously in England. They also saw the college as a feeder for clergymen who would perpetuate their Puritan beliefs. Historian Samuel Eliot Morrison wrote that more than half of Harvard's seventeenth century graduates became ministers.

Though many believe that Harvard College was founded by John Harvard, this is only partially true. John Harvard was an English clergyman who arrived in America in 1637, a year after Harvard was founded. He died at age thirty, just a year after his arrival. A wealthy person from an earlier inheritance, Harvard bequeathed half of his estate and his 400-volume library to the college, then named the New College. In tribute of the college's first benefactor, in May of 1639, the general court renamed the college in honor of John Harvard, along with a bronze statue of him that sits in Harvard Yard.

The Latin School-Harvard connection can clearly be seen in the entrance requirements the college set for prospective students as far back as 1642: "When any scholar is able to read Tully (Cicero)...extempore, and make and speak true Latin in verse and prose...and decline perfectly nouns and verbs in the Greek tongue, then may he be admitted into the college."

For the years that followed, eminent graduates with both a Latin School and a Harvard connection would later become historical icons. A long and impressive brag sheet carries names like Samuel Adams and John Hancock; philosophers Ralph Waldo Emerson and George Santayana; religious leaders Cotton Mather and Phillips Brooks; social reformers Charles Sumner, Wendell Phillips, and Henry Ward Beecher; and four Latin School alumni who went on to become Harvard presidents themselves, John Leverett, Samuel Langdon, Edward Everett, and Charles William Eliot.

The common bond between the Latin School and Harvard has endured to this day. Even though centuries have passed since the beginnings of the Latin School-Harvard connection, as of the writing of this book, more Latin School graduates are still admitted each year to the college than from any other private or public school in the country.

THE MEMORABLE MASTERS

Over the years, novelists, filmmakers, and theatrical producers, have given us a mythical image of the English and colonial period schoolmaster—a male figure with graying hair and a long beard, dressed in a black frockcoat, with vest and prominent timepiece hanging, clothes always appearing rumpled and slightly unkempt, and grim and stern-looking. His classroom was as somber as he, with pupils sitting on long, hard wooden benches affixed to desks. The room's only warmth emitted from a fireplace in the rear of the classroom, lit during winter months. At the front of the room there was an elevated platform, or dais, from which the Master would look down upon his students.

A rod of birch twigs also stood beside the Master to remind the boys of who the class's ruling judge and jury was. One might think this picture to be of a fictional creation. Yet in the case of the Latin School, especially with its first Master, indeed it was not. As a sidenote, despite the rigors that pupils were subjected to, schoolmasters would often be fondly remembered and revered by their students—especially when, decades later, one faced adversity or challenge in the real world.

The famous educator Ezekiel Cheever was appointed Master in 1670, the sixth to hold that position. He served with distinction in that role until his death some thirty-eight years later. Cheever was born in 1614 in London. He attended grammar school and graduated from Emanuel College at Cambridge. In 1637, at the age of twenty-three, he immigrated to New England to begin a career as a schoolmaster. Unlike many university graduates who served as teachers while awaiting their ministerial appointments, Cheever saw his as a lifetime profession, as it would prove to be as the decades unfolded.

Before his tenure at the Boston Latin School, Cheever had been New Haven's schoolmaster for twelve years, followed by eleven years in Ipswich, Massachusetts, and then by another nine years in Charlestown. In each institution, he stood out as a highly prominent and respected schoolmaster, not only by earning recognition for his work in the classroom, but also as a leader in community affairs. The moves from city to city appear to have been largely prompted by opportunities and better housing for his family. These relocations would eventually include two wives and twelve children. Cheever was remembered as a man of firmness and conviction in what he believed. He always stood by others who did the same for him.

Now in only its thirty-fifth year, the Latin School selected Cheever to serve as Master. He was to earn double his Charlestown annual salary, amounting to £50, or the equivalent of about $11,000 annual salary today, plus a residence. During his unprecedented tenure, Cheever established himself for his depth of knowledge of Greek and Latin, and more importantly, for the way in which he imparted lessons and knowledge to his pupils. He had published a Latin text, *Accidence*, that was broadly used by schools during his lifetime and following his death, with eighteen editions eventually being published. A stern disciplinarian, Cheever's pupils were said to have premonitions of when the discipline would strike. He would stroke his long, white beard, with successive strokes—faster and faster as the moment of disciplinary action fell. But with this discipline came a deep dedication. As Phillips Brooks noted years later of Cheever:

> [He] became the Master of the Latin School...It was not only to teach Latin. Latin was merely an instrument of life...He prayed with the boys one by one when he had heard their lessons. He not merely educated their minds, but he wrestled for their souls.

Ezekiel Cheever was to live to the ripe old age of ninety-four. While still teaching and following a visit to hear a sermon by one of his most notable pupils, the Reverend Cotton Mather, Cheever died. His funeral was attended by virtually all of Boston's most prestigious citizens—the governor, councilmen, judges, and, of course, dozens of his past and current pupils.

In this colonial era, Cheever would be the first of a long line of memorable Masters at the Latin School, many of whom remind us of some instructor we might have come crossed paths with during our education—that person who, directly or indirectly, had an impact on us that forever changed lives.

TRANSITION TO A NEW CENTURY

The town of Boston celebrated its seventieth birthday in the year 1700. It had grown from a few hundred settlers that existed in 1630, to an estimated seven thousand inhabitants. Its population exceeded that of New York as well as that of Philadelphia. Its economy was also more sizable than either of those other colonial cities.

Industrious Bostonians, with their strong Protestant work ethic, took advantage of their excellent harbor, and used it to build a thriving maritime economy. The harbor had fourteen shipyards and seventy-eight wharves, with a fleet of several hundred seagoing vessels. Fish, lumber, and farm produce were exported to coastal colonial markets, including the triangular Boston-West Indies-English trade routes. Today the Boston waterfront, now a recreation and cultural center, with its Long Wharf, Quincy Market, and Faneuil Hall, stands as a symbol of a maritime economy and early colonial achievements.

Boston also became a center of small manufacturing, providing a vast array of products and services needed by its residents. There were blacksmiths, wheelwrights, and iron workers; spinners, weavers, and tanners; carpenters and joiners. These trades and industries became the foundation for a small but important new middle class—many of whose children would become Latin School students and alumni. At the top of the economic ladder was an aristocratic society comprised of ship owners, builders, and wealthy merchants who no longer lived in clapboard houses like their ancestors.

Instead, they occupied two-story brick or stone houses. Some also had country retreats in surrounding rural towns, including Cambridge and Milton.

The Boston population was quite literate, a function of elementary and grammar school requirements mandated by law in the 1640s. Harvard College continued to provide the community with an educated group of leaders. Samuel Eliot Morison's history of the College indicates that in the year 1700, there were 291 living alumni, two-thirds of whom were theologians, public servants, or schoolmasters. Also in 1700, the Latin School celebrated its sixty-fifth birthday. The school had become an integral part of thriving Boston. Having grown, the school was housed in a new facility. But this was the only thing that was new about the institution. In fact, it's safe to say that the traditions and principles upon which the school were founded have remained unchanged to this day.

As the eighteenth century unfolded in Boston, the Puritan influences on which the city had been founded were declining in importance. There were several reasons for this. First, its current inhabitants represented a third generation of Americans, whose ties to the founders were now slipping away. The new generation was less zealous than the Winthrops and Cottons, both of whom had passed on fifty years earlier. This new generation no longer faced the economic hardships of their parents or grandparents. They were becoming less dependent on religious teachings as the foundation of their work ethic. Puritan values were becoming American values, less rigid and dogmatic. A new Massachusetts Bay Charter in 1691 abolished church membership as a voting requirement. And finally, in the summer of 1692, the excesses of Puritanism came to light with the Salem Witch Trials and its twenty executions.

Given all these significant developments, there is no evidence that the Latin School was ever impacted by any of these changes—neither its educational philosophy curriculum, nor its teaching methods. Though Puritan leaders were influential in the school's founding, they did not establish the school as a religious institution. Yes, prayers were said each morning, and when appropriate during the day. But the founders, and those who followed, did not interject religious instruction into the classroom. No doubt, they believed instruction could take place on the Sabbath, where two sermons usually took place as well as the "Thursday Lecture" held at the meetinghouse, mandatory for every pupil.

From the earliest stages in its history, the Latin School proved its ability to withstand external forces that might potentially interfere with its core values. In many respects, these values were now more deeply rooted in the principles established by the English grammar schools than by Puritan theologians.

By 1700, the Latin School had an increased enrollment, to an estimated 100 students. To handle this increased student body, Master Cheever was assigned an assistant. The town also authorized that a new schoolhouse be built. The existing property, acquired in 1645, would become the Master's residence, and the new building, located on the north side of School Street, a clapboard two-story structure with shingle roof and eight lower and five upper-floor windows, was dedicated to classrooms. There would be three rows of benches on each side of the classrooms, each separating the pupils by what we would now call "grade level." The new facility, finished in 1704, would serve the community for the next forty-four years. These upgrades were a testament to the city's strong and continuing support of the Latin School, its faculty, and pupils. The schoolhouse would be replaced in 1748 with an even larger all-brick schoolhouse. Following Ezekiel Cheever's death in 1708, and for the rest of the colonial period, the school would be headed by Nathaniel Williams, a Master for twenty-six years, and John Lovell, forty-one years—indicative of the long-term continuity and commitment of the school's faculty.

PROMINENT PUPILS

Today, embossed on the upper frieze of the Assembly Hall at the Latin School's current location on Avenue Louis Pasteur are the names of notables who attended the Latin School. Included are eminent scientists, educators, theologians, philosophers, statesmen, businessmen, literary figures, and social activists. There remains one space reserved for another notable. Pupils in each entering class have usually been told, in a somewhat humorous way, that the space could someday bear their name; that is, if they studied hard and followed the long and well-established principles of the Latin School.

Of those names on the wall, fourteen include alumni who entered the school during the colonial period of history. Foremost of these was Benjamin Franklin, who at the age of eight, enrolled in 1714. Franklin's autobiography, as well as the writings of colonial historians, tell us that his father, Joshua, hoped to see Benjamin someday become a minister. This path would start at the Latin School, and move on to Harvard College, which was, for so many boys at that time, a theological training ground. But, after just less than two years at the Latin School, Joshua withdrew his son and placed him in a writing and arithmetic academy. He then took him on as an apprentice in his candle and soap-making shop. It is not clear whether these moves were for economic reasons, or because his father believed his son was not, after all, really suited for the ministry. Benjamin was known to be an imaginative free-thinker, feisty, and a bit irreverent. The young Franklin remained in Boston, working for his father, and then as an apprentice in a brother's print shop.

At that time, a printer was much more than a press operator. He was a writer, journalist, and publisher of a variety of printed materials—newspapers, pamphlets, almanacs, and advertising broadsheets. Franklin gained a lot of varied experience, which would become the basis of his success later in his life.

In September of 1723, at the age of seventeen, Franklin broke away from his Boston brother's hold and moved to Philadelphia. Biographer Walter Isaacson described Franklin at that time as a talented, clever boy, with "personal magnetism, who attracted people who united to help him." After working as an apprentice and printer's helper for a few more years, Franklin set up his own shop, with his people-oriented personality helping him to get the necessary business his shop needed. The shop handled all the types of jobs done by seventeenth-century printers, including the publication of a newspaper, *The Pennsylvania Gazette*, which he started in October of 1729.

In his early years, Franklin became best known for his *Poor Richard's Almanac*. His publication went beyond what other almanacs usually included—weather forecasts, household hints, poems, games, and puzzles. His would contain maxims and sayings built around themes of self-improvement, self-discipline, frugality, moderation, community service, and the work ethic. They were written in a style that was homespun, earthy, practical, and often humorous. Some were written entirely by Franklin; many, he admitted, were modifications of earlier writings by others.

What is significant about Franklin's writings—and relevant to the origins of the Latin School, is that they came at the time when Puritanism was waning in importance in colonial America. Franklin's writings were moral lessons, yet not beholden to religious dogma. They could stand on their own, as an everyman's set of virtues and values. Historian Henry Steele Commager in his book *The American Mind* made the insightful observation that, "In a Franklin, could be merged the virtues of Puritanism, without the defects." Franklin's aphorisms are clearly not profound or poetic. They are common sense. But their subject matter relates to the virtues and values implicit in what we have termed the American Dream. The Latin School can be proud of this son of a candle-maker, who early on in his life helped shape and enrich the Dream with important virtues and values, many of which would also become those of the Latin School itself. Significant also is the fact that his writings and aphorisms are still widely read today. They, like the Latin School, have endured over time.

Over the 141 years of the Latin School's colonial history, the school's important core values and principles remained unchanged—a theme that still echoes today.

CHAPTER IV:

Birth of a Nation

Here once the embattled farmers stood,
And fired the shot heard round the world.

—RALPH WALDO EMERSON

THE EIGHTEENTH CENTURY WAS A significant period for the Latin School. In the first half of the century, the school celebrated its one-hundredth birthday. In the second half, it would be a witness to, and participant in the birth of a new nation.

At mid-century, the school had moved into a new brick structure, located on the south side of School Street. The school was divided into seven classes, with a separate bench assigned to each. Classes started promptly at seven in the morning during summer months, and eight in the morning during winter—mainly to account for the later sunrise. There were one-week vacations at Thanksgiving and Christmas, and three weeks in August. Latin was studied each year, starting with Ezekiel Cheever's text *Accidence.* In the upper classes, there were studies of Caesars Commentaries, Cicero's Orations, the Aeneid, Xenophon, and Homer.

The school's Master was John Lovell, who many alumni agree should be included in any list of the school's most memorable Masters. He held this position for forty-one years, from 1734 to the onset of the American Revolution in 1775. A Latin School and Harvard graduate, he was known as a strict disciplinarian, and dubbed "the pride of Boston parents and the terror of its youth." Many years later, one of his students wrote of his experiences with Lovell. They called Lovell the "Old Gaffer." By his side he had a short-stubbed stick that he used to inflict his punishment—one clap for minor offenses, and four for the most severe. These infractions included, among more serious offenses, not knowing one's lessons, tardiness, skipping school, whispering, cheating, and boisterous behavior. Students from the time recall that Lovell had a dramatic gymnastic style of flourishing before inflicting his punishment. Discipline to him must have had many dimensions—some of them ceremonial.

At mid-century, Boston had a population of about 17,000. Its local economy was also the largest, compared to these other cities—driven largely by its port, and 300 to 400 sailing ships engaged in maritime activity. Up until this time, New England and the other colonies enjoyed a high degree of freedom, self-government, and home rule. Colonial historian Samuel Eliot Morison points out that citizens had, "the exclusive right to tax their constituents, to appoint officials, commission military officers, raise troops and to control them, own schools, churches, and land systems." But by the 1760s this began to change, as the King and Parliament saw it necessary to raise money from the colonies. The French and Indian Wars had just ended, and these conflicts had proven to be expensive for the British. New funds were needed to pay off war debt, cover future costs of the colonial defense, and provide payment to British officials; not to mention the expenses incurred running the colonies. These were not, in the eyes of many historians, unreasonable British demands. But what followed was a series of acts by Parliament, imposing new taxes on the colonies.

REPRESSIVE ACTS AND PROTESTS

The *Stamp Act,* passed in March of 1764, was the first direct tax imposed on the colonists other than customs duties that existed previously. The tax was charged against public documents, licenses, deeds, and newspapers. Though protests and appeals by colonial leaders resulted in the eventual withdrawal of this tariff, it was soon replaced by the *Townshend Acts* of 1767, which set taxes on a wide variety of imports, including tea. The acts were named after the then-British Chancellor of the Exchequer. Protests followed, together with boycotts of imports. Where only a few years earlier, the colonies had been content and quite satisfied with their existence as an imperial colony, that would now change. In March of 1770, a confrontation occurred between citizens and a sentry at the British garrison, resulting in the killing of five Americans—famously known as the Boston Massacre. Then in December of 1773, the Boston Tea Party followed, where colonists, disguised as Native Mohawks, boarded three docked vessels, and dumped 90,000 pounds of tea into Boston Harbor.

Anger over the Boston Tea Party resulted in Parliament quickly passing the *Coercive, or Intolerable Acts,* calling for a complete blockade of the Boston port, and the quartering of British troops in private homes. The colonists' response to these measures now took a different path, with the calling of the First Continental Congress in September of 1774. The session would be attended by fifty-five delegates from twelve of the thirteen colonies. Its objective was to plan a coordinated response to the British actions.

Latin School alumni played a prominent role in these events. Their involvement began with simple schoolboy protests. In January of 1775, a servant of the British General Haldimand's house spread ashes on a hill used for sledding by the Latin School boys. Records show the lads, "made a muster, and chose a committee to wait upon the General, who admitted them, heard their complaints, and ordered his servant to repair the damage." This was a relatively mild protest compared to what their older Latin School alumni would now do as leaders fomenting a revolution.

LATIN SCHOOL: A FEEDER FOR DEMOCRACY

One of the more memorable and contemporary Masters of the Latin School was Phillip Marson, a highly respected Master who retired in 1957. In retirement, Marson authored three books about the school and his many years of teaching. One of these books was entitled *Breeder of Democracy*, published in 1963. In it, the author posited that, "Little did the Puritan fathers realize that in establishing the Boston Latin School in 1635, and Harvard College a year later, that they were constructing cradles of democracy."

Marson's belief was that public education, and specifically a Latin School type education, was an incubator of democracy. It instilled wisdom of the great philosophers and exposure to different political systems. It taught one how to study, understand, and debate important public issues. It forged language, writing, and verbal skills that could be used to communicate points of view to others. Yet ironically, he explained, early New England had been founded as a theocracy, not a democracy. The Puritan founders of the Latin School, and others who followed, were essentially theocrats—embodying qualities like being rigid, dogmatic, and somewhat intolerant.

Regardless of these traits, and unwittingly in establishing public schools for their children, they were paving the way for their theocracy to become a democracy. The Latin School students of the pre-revolutionary era learned their lessons well. The school was where revolutionists Samuel Adams and John Hancock got their education, as did three others who were signers of the Declaration of Independence.

LATIN SCHOOL REVOLUTIONISTS

Most historians agree that in the events leading up to the Revolutionary War, there were two individuals who played a central role in bringing it about. These individuals were Samuel Adams and John Hancock. Both were from New England, the center of the pre-revolutionary events; both were Boston Latin School graduates, who worked closely together in fueling the revolution.

Samuel Adams

Samuel Adams was born in Boston in 1733, a second cousin of John Adams, the nation's second president. He was the son of a merchant and shipowner, who also owned a brewery. Samuel entered the Latin School at the age of seven and spent a full seven years at the school. He then went on to Harvard College, from which he graduated in 1740, along with twenty-three classmates. After graduation, he entered the family businesses, eventually taking them over upon his father's death. Young Adams was not a good businessman. Each of his businesses failed or ended up going bankrupt, leaving him with little in the way of income to support a family. His *modus operandi* was to take a position in the local government, as one of several elected tax collectors. He did this for nine years, and, as in his past business career, also did not perform very well failing to collect all the taxes he should have. This eventually led to legal action against him by the Massachusetts government.

Adams left the tax collector's job in 1764, at the age of forty-one. His departure was a timely one, as it enabled him to start a new career for which he was better suited: that of political activist. He would soon become a leading figure in the protests of the series of tax acts that the British Parliament had begun to impose on the colonies. The first of these was the *Stamp Act* that had been enacted in 1765 to levy taxes on the colonialists. For the next ten years, Adams would devote all his time in getting the various acts repealed and, in the process, become a leader in sparking the American Revolution.

If a handbook were ever to be written on how to start a revolution, Adams would be its author. He used virtually every tool at his disposal to further the course of liberty, freedom, and independence from England. These tools included newspaper articles under different pen names, propaganda pamphlets, contacts with protest groups in other colonies, recruitment of influential and moneyed supporters, street demonstrations, town hall rallies, and effigy burnings. He was also influential in organizing at least four political activist groups, the best known of which was the Sons of Liberty, largely responsible for the Boston Tea Party. Both the scope and intensity of his activities were unequaled. He did everything short of engaging in violence and bloodshed.

All of Adams's efforts were characterized by presenting powerful emotional arguments—skills learned at the Latin School. He knew he could draw more support by appealing to the emotional needs and concerns of the colonists. Although logic would be the province of Thomas Paine, the approach Adams used to achieve independence was more akin to that of his Virginia counterpart, Patrick Henry, who is remembered in the history books for his famous utterance, "Give me liberty, or give me death." Historians have not been reluctant to portray Adams and his personality with fiery descriptions. He has been termed a radical, a firebrand, a rabble-rouser, inflammatory, a rebel, and a ringleader. But despite these traits, contemporaries all respected him and his accomplishments. Thomas Jefferson later said of him, "For depth of purpose, zeal and sagacity, no man exceeded, if any equaled, Sam Adams." He considered him, "truly the man of the revolution."

John Hancock

John Hancock can be considered the second man of the Revolution. For it was Hancock who joined with Adams and financed much of the protest and rebellious actions that Adams undertook. The British considered Adams and Hancock co-conspirators. In January 1774, two months after the Boston Tea Party, the British attorney general charged Adams and Hancock, along with two others, with high treason and misdemeanors, ordering their arrest and trial.

Hancock was born in 1737 in Braintree, a town just outside of Boston. When he was eight years old, he was enrolled in the Latin School, where he spent five years studying under the eyes of Master John Lovell. Upon graduation from Harvard in 1754, he joined his family's conglomerate of businesses. It included shipping, exports, real estate, and banking. It was known as the House of Hancock. At the age of twenty-seven, with the death of his uncle, John Hancock inherited the businesses, making him one of the richest men in the colonies. A year later, in 1765, the *Stamp Act* came into being. It quickly triggered Hancock's involvement in protest activities along with other Boston merchants. The *Stamp Act,* and the similar Acts to follow, would have a direct economic impact on Hancock's businesses. Some believe that this was the primary reason for his joining the protest movement—more so than for patriotic reasons. Regardless of his motives, John Hancock joined with Sam Adams, and others, in seeking repeal of British tax initiatives. Hancock would now lend his name, prestige, and financial support to that cause.

Hancock was quite different from Sam Adams, who was fifteen years his senior. Hancock was more logical, moderate, restrained, and composed than Adams. While Adams failed in business, Hancock was quite successful at it. Hancock was an aristocrat, who enjoyed a fine home, gilded coaches, and possessions bearing the family coat-of-arms. Adams had no wealth to speak of. When he went as a representative to the First Continental Congress in 1774, his supporters gave him a new suit, shirt, and shoes. What Hancock and Adams may have had most in common was their Latin School-Harvard education. In line with the Marson thesis of the Latin school being an incubator of democracy, Adams's and Hancock's education certainly must have contributed to their understanding of their beliefs and principles, and what drove them to be revolutionaries in the literal sense of the word. With Adams's tenacity, and Hancock's financial prowess, these two very different individuals became partners in the move toward democracy.

THE SHOT HEARD "'ROUND THE WORLD"

On the night of April 18, 1775, Samuel Adams and John Hancock were both in Lexington, a small village northwest of Boston. This was the site of the Massachusetts Provincial Congress, a colony-wide activist group in which they were both involved. Their presence in Lexington was also no doubt prompted by safety concerns, as both were being sought by the British authorities in Boston.

Adams and Hancock were staying at the parsonage home of Reverend Jonas Clarke, a cousin of Hancock's. That evening, they were asleep in the downstairs parlor bedroom. Outside the door was a small contingent from the local militia, there to protect these two patriots. After a knock on the door, a man wearing spurs and heavy riding boots entered the house. His name was none other than Paul Revere, a Boston silversmith, whom both Adams and Hancock knew from their mutual involvement in patriot protest activities. Earlier in the evening, Revere had been asked to ride from Boston to Lexington with a warning that British troops had mustered in Boston and were on their way to Lexington. This is what history has since recorded as the famous, "Ride of Paul Revere."

There are extensive records of what transpired on that iconic night, and the days following. Revere and others gave depositions to the Massachusetts Provincial Congress, as part of the group's investigation of the Lexington-Concord events. In Revere's deposition, he said he was asked,

> To go to Lexington, and inform Mr. Samuel Adams, and the Honorable John Hancock, Esq., that there was a number of soldiers ... marching to the bottom of the [Boston] Common ... It was supposed that they were going to Lexington...to take them, or go to Concord, to destroy Colony stores.

In most historical interpretations of Paul Revere's ride, there is little mention of Adams and Hancock as the primary or even secondary motives for the British march. The Revere depositions show that in route to Lexington, he did alert those in the towns through which he passed. But this was not the primary purpose of his trip. His first stop was at the Clarke parsonage to meet with Adams and Hancock. Then, as a group, the three met with members of the local militia. In an extensively researched book, *Paul Revere's Ride*, by historian David Hackett Fischer, the author tells that,

> Paul Revere's primary mission was not to alarm the countryside. His purpose was to warn Samuel Adams and John Hancock, who were thought to be objects of the expedition. Concord and its military stores were also mentioned to Revere, but only in a secondary way.

As further evidence of the British focus on the importance and where-abouts of Adams and Hancock, two months after the Concord and Lexington battles, British Governor General Thomas Gage issued an amnesty order "promising pardon to all who would lay down their arms–that is, with the exception of Samuel Adams and John Hancock."

In the early morning hours of April 19, 1775, Adams and Hancock visited the Lexington Green, but both they and their supporters agreed that they should return to the Clarke parsonage and remain in hiding and away from any coming battle. What followed at sunrise on that morning is known to everyone. The story of Lexington and Concord was felicitously illustrated in this memorable poem:

By the rude bridge that arched the flood,
Their flag to April's breeze unfurled,
Here once the embattled farmers stood,
And fired the shot heard round the world.
The foe long since in silence slept;
Alike the conqueror silent sleeps;
And Time the ruined bridge has swept
Down the dark stream which seaward creeps.
On this green bank, by this soft stream,
We set to-day a votive stone;
That memory may their deed redeem,
When, like our sires, our sons are gone.
Spirit, that made those heroes dare,
To die, and leave their children free,
Bid Time and Nature gently spare
The shaft we raise to them and thee.

The poem is, as many might recognize, the *Concord Hymn*, written by Ralph Waldo Emerson some sixty years later. It is ironic that Emerson, like the patriots Adams and Hancock, who brought on the war, was also a Latin School graduate, class of 1817. Two sons of the Latin School were the war's instigators, with the first shots commemorated by a Latin School essayist and poet.

On that same morning back in Boston, when Latin School boys went to their classrooms, Master John Lovell was there to announce, "War's begun and school's done ... *deponite libros*," or translated, "*Put away your books*." The school was not to reopen until June 5, 1776, following the British evacuation of Boston. Schoolmaster Lovell, a firm British loyalist, left Boston with the troops. He settled in Halifax and died in 1778. It's kind of poetic that the two most important of the revolutionists, Adams, and Hancock, both studied under Lovell, a staunch Tory loyalist. Though Lovell might not have realized it, his own classroom had truly become a breeding ground for democracy.

THE DECLARATION OF INDEPENDENCE—LAYING THE GROUND FOR THE AMERICAN DREAM

The American Dream had its roots in the Puritan settlements of New England, where the virtues of hard work and self-discipline became part of every child's education. The Latin School founders, Masters, and pupils all helped to create and foster this dream in the colonial period of our history. An important building block in the creation of this dream was the Declaration of Independence, in which Latin School alumni were also deeply involved. Samuel Adams, John Hancock, and Benjamin Franklin are the most prominent of these. On July 4, 1776, they, along with two other Latin School alumni, became signers of the Declaration of Independence. The Latin School can be proud of them.

Two other Latin School figures, perhaps of less notoriety than their fellow alumni, were Robert Treat Paine and William Hooper. Paine began his career as an attorney and patriot, serving as the prosecutor in the Boston Massacre trial of British Captain Thomas Preston. He was a delegate to the First Continental Congress in 1775 and served with distinction on the Massachusetts General Court. Hooper, though also a Latin School graduate, moved to North Carolina, where he was active in its colonial government. The formative years for each of these men were essentially similar—up to six years at the Latin School and four at Harvard. Four of the five men, Franklin excluded, all attended Harvard after Latin School graduation. Though historical records are incomplete, it appears that Hancock and Hooper may have sat in the same Latin School classroom together. Hancock and Paine's attendance may have also overlapped.

As adults, the five Latin School signers must have all known each other well. Except for Franklin, they were generally all in the same age group, thirty-four to fifty-four. Franklin was seventy years of age. Though Franklin was representing Pennsylvania and Hooper, North Carolina, each as a representative at the two Continental Congresses, they all certainly participated in meetings together: Three of the five were delegates at the First Continental Congress in September of 1774; four of five, at the Second Congress in May of 1775. It was from this latter Congress that a five-man committee was formed to prepare an independence document. Franklin was one of its members.

The final published document bears the very striking and bold signature of John Hancock. It reflects the superb penmanship that he, no doubt, learned while at the Latin School. It's worth pointing out that at the end of each day, the Latin School boys were required to attend the South Writing School, where penmanship was taught. Hancock was the first to sign, as he was President of the Continental Congress. The fifty-six signatures are grouped by state, in North to South order, beginning with New Hampshire's three signatories. This is followed by the Massachusetts group, the first of whom is Samuel Adams. Historians offer no explanation as to why Samuel's signature precedes that of John Adams.

The Adams-Hancock story does not end with the signing of the Declaration of Independence. After the war, both men went on to serve as Massachusetts governors. Both were instrumental in the 1788 ratification of the U.S. Constitution. John Hancock, though younger than Adams, died at the age of fifty-seven in 1793. Adams died a decade later at the age of eighty-one.

Over the years, Samuel Adams' legacy has been overwhelmed by the reputation and attention given to his cousin, John Adams. Perhaps this is because Samuel never held a major national office, and only state positions.

Another theory may be that he was a rebel and a maverick, whose image may not have fit the statesman's imagery that we envision in national leaders.

Today, Samuel is the better-known Adams in Boston. Some say it is because of the beer company that markets a microbrew bearing his name. For others, it's because of the large statue displayed behind Faneuil Hall, where so many times he had aroused citizens of the city at his fiery rallies. This ten-foot-tall bronze statue of Adams, standing erect, with arms folded and visited by tourists each year, is inscribed, "Samuel Adams 1722-1803—A Patriot—He organized the Revolution, and signed the Declaration of Independence. Governor—A True Leader of the People" ... and Latin School alumnus.

CHAPTER V:

Nineteenth-Century Continuity Amidst Change

"The art of progress is to preserve order amid change and to preserve change amid order."

—ALFRED NORTH WHITEHEAD

IN 1800, THE NEW AMERICAN nation was nearing its twenty-fifth birthday, while the Latin school was celebrating its 165th. Thomas Jefferson had just been elected president, replacing New England's John Adams. The new census showed the nation's population at 5.3 million people. The country's geographic area now extended well beyond the original coastal colonies, all the way west to the Mississippi River.

Massachusetts, incorporated as a commonwealth in 1780, had its seat of government in Boston, in a newly constructed brick building at the crest of Beacon Hill. It had been designed by Charles Bulfinch, a prominent Boston architect and Latin School graduate. Bulfinch would oversee the renovation and enlargement of Faneuil Hall. In the new statehouse, the governor was Caleb Strong, a fifty-five-year-old Harvard-educated lawyer. Strong was a

Federalist and had served as a delegate at the Continental Convention in 1787, and later as a U.S. senator.

At the turn of the century, Boston was still a relatively small town. Its population was just under 25,000 compared with New York's 60,000 and Philadelphia's 41,000. Boston would not be incorporated as a city until 1822. Local industry continued to be tied to its port activities, though there were several small factories emerging in outlying areas near the water, including Lowell and Lawrence, where power could be drawn from the Merrimack River.

Around this time, the Latin School's enrollment was around 125 students. The Master was Samuel Hunt, who had been appointed when classes resumed after the British evacuation of Boston in June of 1776, following John Lovell's abdication. Students still occupied the schoolhouse constructed in 1748, the school's third building to be erected. Destroyed by a fire in 1812, it was then replaced by a new granite structure at the same location.

The Latin School curriculum, administration, and other administrative matters were now governed by a new set of town guidelines, issued in October 1789. These guidelines were defined as the "New System of Public Education." They were drafted by a town committee that included Latin School alumnus Samuel Adams. This new governance included a reduction of the Latin School curriculum from seven to four years, with admission beginning at ten years of age, a new curriculum, and textbooks. There would be three writing and three reading schools in the town that students were required to attend prior to Latin School entry. Arithmetic would be taught at these schools. School hours and holidays were clearly delineated. Four committees were established to oversee and inspect the schools on a regular basis. Not covered under the new program was elementary school education, which would not be dealt with in any major way for another few decades. Home-schooling or private tutoring of younger children was considered an adequate solution.

GATEWAY TO OPPORTUNITY: THE CHALLENGE OF CHANGE

Historians who have carefully studied nineteenth century America characterize the period as one in which far-reaching changes took place. By century's end, the nation's land mass had reached from the Atlantic to the Pacific Ocean. The frontier had closed, with a transcontinental railroad now connecting coasts. By 1900, the U.S. population had reached 76.2 million, up from the modest 5.3 million when the century began. The industrial age had also arrived, spawning new breakthroughs in science and technology. The women's movement got its start at mid-century, when social activist Elizabeth Cady Stanton organized a New York State conference. And there was, of course, the Civil War that divided the nation. In education, new thinkers including Horace Mann, Henry Barnard, and John Dewey came onto the scene. High schools were now open in virtually every community in the country. All states had new land-grant colleges, giving low-cost access to higher education to the nation's youth.

Along with this rapid change, the city of Boston, which was incorporated in 1822, saw its population mushroom to 561,000 by the year 1900. Normal population growth, immigration, and the acquisition of almost a dozen nearby towns contributed to this sizable increase. With a high level of immigration in the second half of the new century, the ethnic mix of the city also began to dramatically change. A 1900 census showed that 35 percent of the city's residents were foreign born, largely from Ireland. The city's economy transformed as well, from one dependent on the sea trade, to one more diversified in manufacturing, commerce, and financial services.

It is in the context of this dramatically transformed environment that one would expect the Boston Latin School to experience significant change as well. In fact, there remained a high degree of continuity with the core principles of the school. Yes, there were refinements and adjustments along the way. But as far as any major changes, there were very few to speak of at the school. To borrow a seafaring analogy apropos of Boston sailing ships during trans-Atlantic crossings—they might experience severe storms. They might veer temporarily off course, their masts and rigging likely incurring damage. However, the vessels arrived safely in port, guided by solid purpose and skilled and committed captains. Once in port, the ships required repairs, but would soon sail again, because they were well-engineered and constructed with future voyages in mind.

For the Latin School, there too were to be stormy seas. But, as with all seafaring vessels, the school weathered the storms with skill and proficiency. The only noticeable changes were that of the school's physical blueprint, enlarged to accommodate students from a more sizable Boston population base. What did not veer off course was the school's core classical curriculum, the virtues and values instilled in its pupils, and the teaching discipline and leadership commitments of its faculty.

CURRICULUM CONTINUITY

The Latin School curriculum in the first half of the century can be best described by a prominent pupil of the school, Charles William Eliot, one of his generation's most respected educators and a long-time Harvard president. He spoke at the Latin School's 275th anniversary in 1910, addressing attendees with the following words:

> Sixty-six years ago [1844], when I entered it [the Latin School], the subjects of instruction were Latin, Greek, mathematics, English composition and declamation, and the elements of Greek and Roman history. There was no formal instruction in the English language and literature, no modern language, no science, and no physical training, or military drill. In short, the subjects of instruction were what they had been for two hundred years.

It's difficult to know for certain whether this opening address was a criticism or compliment of the Latin School. Perhaps it was a bit of both. But this much is known: it was not until 1852 that some changes in the curriculum began to take place, and these were only minor in nature. In that year's school catalog, English grammar first appeared as a continuing requirement, starting in Grade 7 (Class VI); English composition in Grade 9 (Class IV).

As for modern languages, French was listed for study beginning in Class IV. It was, at that time and still today, considered the language of international relations and diplomacy. Latin School's Benjamin Franklin was fluent in French, representing the colonies in Paris. *Lingua franca* was also seen as a language of elite and educated Europeans for the study and appreciation of French literature and art. German did not appear in the school's catalog listing until 1870, probably added in recognition of the extensive scholarly research taking place at German universities.

Other than these few changes, the core curriculum continued to be built on the principles of a classical education, the foundation of which was Latin—Caesar's Commentaries, Cicero's Orations, Virgil, and others. Latin began in Class VI and continued through Class I. Ancient Greek was taught in Class IV thru Class I. Studies in the sciences during this period were still limited to geography, added in 1814. As for the natural sciences, none would be included in the curriculum until 1870s. By that year, the Latin School had largely held to its core curriculum for 235 years. It was at this time that the Boston School Committee decided to examine the curriculum, and its adequacy in educating Boston's future citizens.

One of the individuals who would play a role in the curriculum reexamination, and mentioned earlier, was Charles William Eliot, one of four Latin School graduates who later became Harvard presidents. Eliot served as the Harvard president from 1869 until 1908. During his 39-year tenure, he literally defined what a liberal arts education should be. His influence as an educator was felt at every level of schooling. Earlier in his career, he had taught mathematics and chemistry, studied the European lycée and gymnasium school systems, and published numerous works on his philosophy of education. As an active Latin School alumnus, he was called upon regularly for counsel and advice by the Boston School Committee. In 1868, he was, "asked to appear at Committee hearings to which eminent educators are to be invited" to discuss possible changes in the role of the Latin School in a changing Boston community.

Another individual who would be involved with the Committee was the school's then Head Master, Francis Gardner. Like Eliot, he was also Latin School and Harvard-educated. Gardner was twenty-two years older than Eliot and was a Sub-Master at the school during the time Eliot was a student. One perhaps learned from the other. Gardner was appointed Head Master in 1851, and served in that position for twenty-five years. Before his appointment, he had taught at the school for twenty years as an Usher, Sub-Master, and Master.

In 1868, Gardner found himself amid a controversy in the role of the Latin School. The School Committee, and others, began questioning the Latin School's continued adherence to its rigid classical curriculum in a time when the world around it was changing so rapidly, especially as the country was becoming more industrialized. So, should the school continue to be a college preparatory school? Or should it dutifully prepare its graduates for occupations that may or may not require a college education? Hearings were conducted to address this issue, and outside expertise was solicited. Proposals were reviewed that included closing the Latin School entirely, merging it with the English High School, or making major changes in the current curriculum.

What was finally agreed to by the School Committee in the summer of 1870 was what they called "a new general broad culture curriculum" for the Latin School—or better phrased, a "hodgepodge" for a solution. New subjects would be added to the existing curriculum, including zoology, geology, botany, chemistry, and astronomy, as well as drawing, music, and gymnastics. The intent of the reformers was certainly well intentioned, but the result would prove to be impracticable, confusing, unfocused, and difficult to administer. It would also reduce the time devoted by the students to their classical studies. Within a year, the curriculum was modified and in 1876 eliminated in its entirety.

What replaced the 1870 curriculum, however, was one that did incorporate some new courses of study but did so without diluting the classical studies curriculum that has remained a hallmark of the Latin School. Charles William Eliot's advice was for a more modern and balanced curriculum that now included the natural sciences, history, math, grammar and literature, and modern languages. The replacement curriculum, adopted in 1876, became the new standard for the school, and it would remain virtually unchanged well into the next century. The Latin School had weathered a storm. It was built to last.

Shortly after the new 1876 curriculum was adopted, a local journalist commented on what had transpired, and what lay ahead in this way:

> It will be seen that 1876 begins a new era in the history Boston's most venerable and most celebrated literary institution. It has been most wisely decided to continue it as a distinctly classical preparatory school, with a new and improved curriculum. This course is to be pursued not with reference to educating the pupil for business.

> The work of the Latin School is to prepare the student to enter college with the kind of instruction which shall best enable him to pursue a college course. In a word, its work is to feed the professions, and so long as Boston needs clergymen, doctors, and lawyers, it is right and proper that she should see to it that a *free* school is provided, so that her humblest citizen may secure to his children a classical, college education, and that poverty may be no insurmountable obstacle of talent.

The year 1876 was also significant for the school in another respect. Like memorable Master Ezekiel Cheever in the prior century, Francis Gardner died while Head Master. Gardner had given 45 years of service to the school. At his funeral, one of his pupils remembered him fondly:

> Thorough and systematic in his instruction, he trained his pupils in good habits of study, mental accuracy, and solid foundations of learning ... No one could hear him conduct a recitation in Homer without

seeing how minute was his knowledge, and how careful had been his study of Greek.

Shortly after Gardner's death, Moses Merrill became Head Master. Like Gardner, Merrill's tenure would be a lengthy one—43 years, with 34 as Head Master. The school now had 430 pupils taught by the Head Master, three Masters, six Sub-Masters, and three so-called Ushers, or junior faculty members. The lengthy and back-to-back tenures of Gardner and Merrill are another example of the school's ability to maintain continuity. We witnessed this continuity in the curriculum, and in the school's faculty as well.

EARLY-DAY DIVERSITY

Despite the challenges to the Latin School curriculum that transpired in the late 1870s, the School Committee continued its support for the school by committing what would be equivalent to $20 million today, for the construction of a new facility. With these funds, a schoolhouse would be erected on Warren Avenue and Montgomery Street in the South End of Boston. The Latin School would occupy one side of the building, the English High School, the other. The classrooms and the student bodies would be kept separate, and each school would have its own entrance.

A combined facility was no doubt decided upon to save on construction costs. The decision must also have been a post-1870s reaffirmation that the two schools could co-exist, side by side, each serving the different needs of Boston's residents—one school with a classical curriculum for college preparation, and one with a non-classical curriculum to provide broader education to prepare students for the practical skills required for commerce and business.

When completed in 1880, the new building was termed, "the largest structure in America devoted to education purposes, and the largest in the world as a free public school." The structure was three stories in height, with a basement constructed in a Renaissance style of brick and stone. The Latin School had twenty-four classrooms of its own, seating up to thirty-six pupils. In addition, on the second floor, there was a lab room for teaching physics and chemistry, and a 200-seat lecture hall with learning-aid display cases. As the sixth schoolhouse over the course of the school's history, the Warren Avenue facility would be the home of a growing Latin School into the twentieth century.

No available data on the socio-economic or ethnic makeup of the students exist from this time, but some are available for the Boston population. The city appears to have been composed of four groups. At the very top were the affluent, aristocratic, "old money" Boston Brahmins, many of whom were the direct descendants of English colonialists. Next in line was the upper middle-class group, who were merchants, shopkeepers, and white-collar workers. This was followed by blue-collar, or middle-class groups of skilled artisans that included carpenters, masons, painters, tailors, and shoemakers. At the fourth and lowest in the ranks were the common laborers and domestic servants.

To answer the question as to which socio-economic groups sent the greatest proportion of their sons to the Latin School, we can start with a premise that has held up until this day: the higher up the family is on the socio-economic ladder, the greater the likelihood that their offspring would attend college. This premise logically can then be extended to the likelihood of attending a college preparatory school, such as the Latin School.

The term Brahmin was coined by the physician and writer Oliver Wendell Holmes, Sr. in an 1860 novel. He borrowed the term from India. It was used to define the Hindus highest and most priestly class. In nineteenth-century Boston, the Brahmins were the ruling class, by virtue of wealth acquired during the colonial years, their university educations, and positions of political power. A famous poem by John Collins Bossidy best sums up their status in this way:

And this is good old Boston,
The home of the bean and the cod,
Where the Lowells talk to the Cabots
And the Cabots talk only to God.

Criticism of the Boston Brahmins focused on the incongruous nature of this aristocratic group in this new democratic society—a society which their ancestors helped create. On one hand, they looked down on anyone beneath them, particularly new immigrants. On another hand, others would argue that they created a cultural environment for Boston that made it the Athens of America. This was done through their philanthropic gifts in support of education, libraries, and museums. One of these philanthropists was Henry Lee Higginson, an 1851 Latin School graduate, who founded the Boston Symphony Orchestra and funded the construction of Symphony Hall. He was a wealthy banker. He was also a major Harvard benefactor, where he paid for the construction of the Harvard Union Student Center. In 1890, he also gave Harvard thirty-one acres of land. It was to become Soldiers' Field, in honor of seven friends he had lost in the Civil War. Higginson had been a cavalry major and was wounded in the war.

There were other Brahmins of prominence in Boston's nineteenth-century history. Many of their names appear in the roster of students at the Latin School during the period. The lists suggest that this top socio-economic group, more so than others, sent their sons to the school. Latin School historian Henry Jenks, in a work written in 1876, shares a list of students organized by family name. A quick account shows the Adams name appears thirty-four times during the nineteenth century; Shaw, fifteen; Gardner, twelve; Cabot, ten; Appleton, nine; and Lowell, six.

Despite this abundance of both affluence and influence, a conclusion should not necessarily be drawn that the Brahmins were the exclusive and only source of Latin School pupils. By the nineteenth century, Brahmin parents had other new and prestigious preparatory college options available to them including Phillips Andover, Phillips Exeter, and the Deerfield

Academy. Each of these private schools also had strong ties to Harvard and the other seven Ivy League colleges where many Brahmin boys were eventually enrolled.

Two middle-class groups served as feeders to the Latin School. These included middle-class merchants, shopkeepers, white-collar workers, and the blue-collar, middle-class skilled artisans. Though most parents in these groups had not attended college, the availability of the Latin School as a *free* and *public* college preparatory school gave their children opportunities they didn't have. For them, the Latin School served as a gateway of opportunity, enabling their offspring to do better and go further in life. Although no reliable enrollment data exist among the population of students that were from middle-class families, it can be assumed that many of these pupils moved up the economic ladder.

These same opportunities, however, did not exist for immigrants at the bottom of the economic ladder—among them the common or unskilled laborers and domestic servants for whom work was often sporadic. These low-paid groups accounted for approximately 25 to 30 percent of the Boston working population. Most of these were Irish immigrants who began coming to Boston in 1846 to escape the potato crop failure and famine that struck their homeland. Data gathered by immigrant historian Oscar Handlin show that Boston port arrivals from Ireland in just a ten-year period between 1846 and 1856 reached almost 130,000. Though many of them settled in areas surrounding Boston, the impact on the ethnic makeup of the city was a sizable one.

New immigrants to the Boston area were largely uneducated, and without occupational skills. Most had been peasant farmers. As a result, they were forced to take the lowest paying jobs, if they could find them. In 1850, the ethnic Irish accounted for a third of the Boston workforce, but a disproportionate two-thirds of laborers and domestic servants. By 1880, though there was a modest improvement in their status, the Irish still accounted for half of the employment in these low-pay categories.

Though education was made compulsory in Massachusetts in 1852, many of the children of the Irish immigrants were to be found working, rather than in school. Economic necessity forced their sons and daughters to support the sporadic wages of their parents. Even for these young people, steady jobs were hard to find. Discriminatory practices were widespread, with advertisements stating, "No Irish Need Apply." Immigrant parents themselves, unfortunately, also restricted educational opportunities for their sons and daughters. Many opposed public education, believing it to be the responsibility of their Catholic Church, rather than the state. Parochial schools were thus opened but were limited in number and the quality of education provided.

It's not surprising, therefore, that very few boys from this lowest socio-economic class would attend the Latin School. The Henry Jenks rosters of students lists very few Irish names—as late as 1875, or even twenty-five years after the peak years of Irish immigration. It wasn't until the twentieth century that the Irish would begin to achieve upward mobility and the rosters of Latin School and their Masters would be populated with Irish surnames.

PROMINENT PUPILS

The nineteenth century Latin School continued to produce a long list of prominent pupils. Today, the Latin School Assembly Hall upper frieze displays the names of twenty-one individuals whose prominence and impact were felt in the nineteenth century. They include, among others, Ralph Waldo Emerson, Edward Everett Hale, Charles William Eliot, Phillip Brooks, Henry Lee Higginson, and Charles Francis Adams.

Among the century's most notable alumni were two individuals—both of whom shared a common set of values and beliefs reflecting one of the integral parts of the Latin School's core values: *equality of opportunity*. These individuals were Wendell Phillips and Charles Sumner. Both were leaders of the abolitionist movement in the mid-nineteenth century. The two had several things in common. They were of the same age, both born in 1811. They both attended the Latin School at the same time and then attended Harvard together. By all accounts, they were close friends, and continued to Harvard Law School to become lawyers.

Phillips and Sumner gained fame in large part due to their oratory skills and set out to convince Americans that slavery must be abolished. Though it is not known for certain how or when they acquired their oratorical skills, there is an interesting historical coincidence. It is that these Latin School graduates had both studied under Benjamin Apthorp Gould, the Master who in about 1814, added declamation—a rhetorical exercise in which the combined use of eloquent language and effective oral delivery are used to inform, persuade, or motivate an audience—to the Latin School curriculum. Students were required to "declaim" once a month, and each Saturday convene as a group to hear their classmates' presentations. To this day, declamation remains a part of the school's requirements.

In the exercise of declamation, students select and prepare an oration on a subject of historical or ethical importance. This may involve arguing both sides of an issue, and sometimes impersonation of the protagonists. The language used is to be eloquent and inspirational, appealing to both the hearts and minds of the audience. Delivery is key and relies on voice, diction, and gestures. This type of training dates to Aristotle in the fourth century B.C. Although our two abolitionists had much in common, they were still individuals each with his own distinctive characteristics.

Wendell Phillips

In November of 1811, in a four-story brick mansion on Beacon Hill, Wendell Phillips was born to wealthy Brahmin parents whose ancestors were among Boston's first settlers. At the age of eleven, Phillips was enrolled in the Boston Latin School, located within walking distance of his home. At the time, the school had 225 students, led by its Master, Benjamin Apthorp Gould. It was Gould who introduced declamation into the curriculum, and from whom Phillips most likely learned his basic oratorical skills. Historian and biographer James Brewer Stewart indicates that Phillips won declamation prizes. A classmate remembers him "for his elocution," saying that, "I looked forward to declamation day with interest, mainly on his account." Phillips was also chosen to give his class's salutatory commencement address—completely memorized and all in Latin. His interest in public speaking continued at Harvard, where he studied under the then Professor of Rhetoric and Oratory, Edward T. Channing.

After graduating from Harvard in 1831, Phillips went on to the law school, practicing law in Boston for a few years. He was soon drawn into the abolitionist movement. In December 1837, he attended a Faneuil Hall gathering to condemn the murder of an Illinois abolitionist editor. He spoke eloquently at the rally and found what would become his new calling—actively working for the abolition of slavery. He quickly bonded with William Lloyd Garrison, generally considered the leader of the movement. While Garrison would use his own writings and printing press to gain public support for the movement, it was Phillips who quickly became its major voice.

Phillips was less radical in his approach than most other abolitionists. Many of his counterparts used religion as the basis of their arguments in support of abolition. Phillips, on the other hand, presented his views based on social and political mores—civil liberty, political freedom, social equality, and economic self-determination. He saw the abolitionist movement as "a struggle to finish what our fathers left unfinished," when they declared all men are created equal. He envisioned the abolition of slavery as only one of several steps that had to be taken to achieve racial equality, well before the Emancipation Proclamation ordered the freeing of slaves in states rebellious to the Union. On several occasions he petitioned the Massachusetts legislature to end segregation in public facilities, schools, and transportation. On the latter, he cited the discriminatory practices of the railroads, though serving the public, forced Blacks to ride in segregated seats. History tells us that Phillips was well ahead of his time. A century later, in December of 1955 in Montgomery, Alabama, when a Black woman, Rosa Parks, refused to give up her seat on a city bus, the same issue presented itself.

When the emancipation and constitutional amendments banning slavery finally did come, Phillips was not satisfied. He openly criticized Lincoln for not going far enough to ensure that slavery not only be ended, but that segregation among races cease as well. Phillips was more than an abolitionist. He was an individual who tried to shape the American Dream of equal opportunity for everyone. He can be remembered as a Latin School son who symbolized the same values that the school stood for over the course of its history.

Charles Sumner

Unlike Wendell Phillips, Charles Sumner was born into a family of more modest means. Though his father was an attorney, his practice was limited, making it difficult to provide the kind of income needed to support a wife and nine children. Later in life, his father's fortunes did improve with his appointment as Sheriff for Boston's Suffolk County.

Young Sumner, born in 1811, entered Latin School at age ten. Phillips enrolled a year later. With just over 200 students in the school, it is safe to assume that Phillips and Sumner got to know one another. We do know later during their work in the abolitionist movement, they did become close. Like Phillips, Sumner went on to Harvard College and then to the Law School, graduating in 1834. At each of the institutions he attended, Sumner proved to be an excellent student—particularly in the classics, history, grammar, and rhetoric. Admitted to the bar at age twenty-three, he practiced only briefly. He was interested more in the theoretical aspects of the law, rather than its day-to-day practical aspects. Much of his time was therefore spent in writing and lecturing on legal theory. These activities prompted him to pursue his studies in Europe. Thanks to a loan from wealthy friends, he embarked on a three-year trip with letters of introduction to notable government officials and legal scholars in the countries he would visit. The experience was not only a broadening one for him, but he also returned with a knowledge of French, German, and Italian—unusual for most individuals at the time.

Sumner's first involvement with racial issues came in 1849, when he challenged the legality of segregated schools in Boston. Though he lost his case, six years later the state legislature outlawed racial segregation in all public schools. His fame was to come later as a United States senator in support of the abolitionist cause. Whereas his friend Wendell Phillips would present his arguments in public venues, Sumner became the movement's leading spokesman in the halls and corridors of government. Elected by the Massachusetts legislature to the Senate in 1851, he would use his unbounded energy and oratorical skills to argue vigorously for the end of slavery.

Sumner had learned and applied his rhetorical and oratorical skills well at the Latin School in declamation. Sumner's speeches were all well prepared, with their key points backed by facts and statistics. Each speech had a clear beginning, middle, and end. Although they were all quite lengthy, he memorized and rehearsed each one of them. His language tended to be somewhat florid, and usually included Latin quotations. His impassioned delivery was enhanced by his physical presence of six feet-and-two inches in height, and his dress was just as impressive.

Historian and Sumner biographer David Donald cites the orator's numerous speeches as milestone events. Most famous of these was his May 1856, *The Crime Against Kansas* speech, in which he outlined what he saw as the evils associated with allowing slavery in the new Kansas-Nebraska Territory. It was three hours in length, with tough, intimidating language that infuriated southern senators. Two days after he delivered the speech, Congressman Preston Brooks from South Carolina entered the Senate chamber where Sumner was sitting at his desk.

He denounced the speech, and then, with his cane, brutally assaulted Sumner, leaving him unconscious and bleeding. The beating resulted in a three-year recovery period for Sumner. The Massachusetts legislature held his absent seat open until he returned in 1859. Historian Bruce Catton remarked years later that, "The assault on Sumner may be regarded as the first blow of the Civil War."

Upon Sumner's return, he resumed his role as the Senate's leading anti-slavery spokesman. His use of scathing language condemning slavery continued in his eloquent and widely reported speeches. In June of 1860, he delivered a 35,000-word oration, calling slavery "barbarous in origin; barbarous in its law; barbarous in all of its pretensions; barbarous in the instruments it employs and its consequences." There was no moderation or compromise in what he had to say, and he spent the balance of his life in the Senate, dying at the age of sixty-three, after twenty-three years of service in government. He is remembered today as a learned scholar and a magnificent orator of undaunted courage in promoting the cause of equal opportunity.

There was a third abolitionist, but one with only a brief Latin School background. This was Henry Ward Beecher, who attended the school for two years in 1826-27. Beecher's family had relocated to Boston from Litchfield, Connecticut, where his father was a minister.

Biographer Debby Applegate tells us that young Beecher was not a very good student at the Latin School, more interested in the sailing ships docked in Boston Harbor than his classical studies. He soon withdrew from the school and was enrolled by his father in a boarding school in Amherst, Massachusetts.

Beecher graduated from Amherst College in 1834, and went on to divinity school, following in the footsteps of his father and seven brothers who also became ministers. His sister, Harriet Beecher Stowe became the most famous member of the twelve children in the family, with her publication of *Uncle Tom's Cabin*.

From the 1850s until his death in 1887, Beecher was recognized as one of the foremost clergymen in support of abolition. Noted for his brilliant and eloquent oratorical skills, he enjoyed the status of a celebrity—asked to speak, and even be compensated for his speeches. Beecher, a pastor of a large Brooklyn church, conducted Sunday sermons that drew crowds as large as 3,000 including notables such as Mark Twain, Walt Whitman, and even Abraham Lincoln. He was chosen by Lincoln to speak at Fort Sumter at the celebration of its recapture by Union troops at the closing of the Civil War. Though the Latin School cannot really take credit for developing the unusual skills that he possessed, Beecher's name is included on the upper frieze in the school's Assembly Hall, not in recognition of what he might have learned there, but what he, like Phillips and Sumner, stood for—equal opportunity for all.

End of a Century

The nineteenth century produced many dramatic events in our nation—economic, political, and social in scope. During this time, Boston, which was home of the Latin School, also changed, growing from a small town to the nation's fifth largest city by the close of the century. What did not change, however, was the Latin School itself—its curriculum, teaching methods, the commitment of its Masters, and its core values. Ironically, amidst all the historical events of the time, many of them the result of the Latin School alumni, the school maintained its identity.

As in earlier periods in history, the eighteenth-century chapter in the Latin School history was characterized by the contribution of prominent pupils who helped shape the American Dream. Wendell Phillips, Charles Sumner, and Henry Ward Beecher were central to this shaping. Their education at the Latin School most certainly must have influenced their lives and the beliefs they held about our country. In their case it was the belief in *equality of opportunity*. This theme will again be even more apparent in the next chapter in history, as the Latin School continued to open its doors of opportunity to the sons and daughters of immigrants who arrived on our shores in the twentieth century.

CHAPTER VI:

Twentieth-Century Student Diversity

"Our flag is red, white, and blue, but our nation is a rainbow—red, yellow, brown, black, and white—and we're all precious in God's sight."

—JESSE JACKSON

IN EACH OF THE LATIN School's remarkable chapters, its graduates played a central role in shaping history, and in promoting what was to be known as the American Dream. Other graduates, less notable, also gained knowledge and values from their Latin School experience that enabled them to fulfill the promises of the Dream—to move up in society and enjoy a better quality of life for themselves and for their offspring.

The Latin School story of the twentieth century is one in which the school and the American Dream were one and the same. As the new century began, the character and makeup of the U.S. population would now undergo dramatic change, as millions of new immigrants flooded to our shores. What drove them here was their pursuit of the Dream. The Latin School, in large part, provided many of these immigrants, and their children, a gateway to opportunity that would enable them, like those before them, to transform the Dream into a living reality.

IMMIGRANTS AND THE AMERICAN DREAM

Among the many factors contributing to the evolution of the American Dream, none was more important than the immigrant experience. Over our country's history, millions emigrated from their homelands, seeking a better life in America for themselves and for their children. But immigration was not an easy or pleasant experience for these individuals. An anonymous quote by an Italian immigrant who passed through Ellis Islands best conveys this sentiment:

> Before I came to America, I thought the streets were paved in gold. When I came here I learned three things: The streets were not paved in gold, the streets weren't paved, and that I was expected to pave them.

The immigration process itself was characterized by extreme personal hardship—leaving one's village, family, and friends; scraping up enough money for the ocean passage, usually enduring crowded steerage accommodations; and, upon landing, undergoing the watchful scrutiny of custom officers, who had the power to deny immigrant entry into the U.S. That would only be the beginning. The next hurdle to face was finding a place to live, and a job that would pay enough to support one's family. Most immigrants would have to settle for low-paying jobs as unskilled laborers.

TURN OF THE CENTURY IMMIGRATION

Between 1890 and 1920, there were 16 million new immigrant arrivals from Europe, or an average of 540,000 per year. This was almost double the annual rate that occurred from 1850 to 1890. There was also a dramatic shift in countries from which these immigrants originated. In the pre-1890 period, more than 85 percent came from Northern Europe. In the 1890-1920 period, this reversed itself, with almost 75 percent now coming from Eastern, Central, and Southern Europe and only 25 percent coming from Northern Europe.

This sizable influx was influenced by several factors. These included political and economic difficulties in the immigrants' homelands, in contrast to the freedom and economic opportunities that existed the U.S. What's more, steamships could now make the ocean crossing in eight to ten days, so ship lines aggressively promoted their services and fares to those contemplating making a new life for themselves abroad.

Irish immigration, which had been so significant following the potato famine in the 1850s, was still sizable, yet at lower annual rates. Despite this falloff, Irish ancestry continued to be the largest non-Anglo ethnic group immigrating to the U.S. Unfortunately, assimilation and upward movement of Boston's Irish immigrants was difficult and lengthy. Some of the sons and daughters of the early Irish immigrants did find better jobs than their parents. While a construction day-laborer may have been the job held by the Irish immigrant father, subsequent generations were starting to do a bit better, moving into more skilled construction occupations such as plumbers, steamfitters, and boilermakers. Others found opportunities as municipal workers—police officers, firefighters, sanitation, or transit workers. There was much less discrimination in these public-sector jobs, as the rising power and influence of Irish politicians helped open these jobs to their constituents. In 1885, Hugh O'Brien became Boston's first Irish mayor. He was followed by three others including John Fitzgerald, a Latin School alumnus.

Italian immigration became the largest single source of new arrivals in the 1890 to 1920 period. Nationally, 2.5 million Italians entered the country, with an annual inflow of 85,000 a year, a tenfold increase from pre-1890 levels. These immigrants were largely poor, unskilled, rural peasants, usually from the distressed regions of Southern Italy. In Boston, and in other cities where they settled, they became day-laborers, building roads, sewers, and transit lines. In Boston, as the Irish moved up the ladder to more skilled and supervisory jobs, the new Italian arrivals filled their previous low-wage, unskilled jobs.

Greek immigrants were the second major source of those arriving from Southern Europe. Though their numbers were smaller—nationally at 12,000 per year—they tended to be a lot more skilled than the Italian immigrants. In Greece, citizens had worked in urban environments and had entrepreneurial skills that enabled them to start small service businesses, including restaurants, laundries, and barber shops.

Jewish immigration to the U.S. in the 1890-1920 period totaled an estimated 2.5 million. Precise numbers are hard to obtain, as both immigration and census data do not record religious affiliation. Immigration historians estimate that 75 percent of the Jewish immigrants came from Russia; the remainder from Germany, Austria, Hungary, Poland, and Romania. The sizable exodus from Russia was prompted by the government's repressive programs that imposed education, occupation, and residency restrictions on Jews. Of the arrivals in the three decades noted, historians agree that the Jewish immigrants were the most literate and skilled. Two thirds of Jewish immigrants had prior skills and commercial experience, particularly in shopkeeping and finance. These immigrants also had a high regard for learning. Literacy and the study of Hebrew was important for the education of their young people. Of all the immigrant groups of this period, Jewish immigrants would achieve the most rapid educational and economic progress.

There is no accurate way to determine the exact number of immigrants in each of the major ethnic groups in Boston during the 1890-1920 period. Although many ethnic groups arrived at the Boston port, others came through New York's Ellis Island, which opened in 1892. Census data exist that shows the foreign-born population residing in Boston in 1920 totaling 243,000, or almost a third of the city's total population.

IMMIGRANT AND OFFSPRING UPWARD MOBILITY (NOT OVERNIGHT)

Social scientists tell us that immigrant assimilation into a new society, and upward mobility, does not happen overnight. Most foreign-born immigrants arrived here with limited education and skills, fluent only in their own language. Low-wage jobs were therefore their only opportunity. The sons or daughters of immigrants, either foreign or native-born here in the U.S., would have more of a chance of overcoming these barriers, assuming that they were not forced to work to supplement their immigrant parents' meager wages. Many children of these immigrants, therefore, enrolled in public elementary and secondary schools, taking their first steps toward upward mobility. In fact, many of the names of these children can be found for the first time in the student rosters at the Boston Latin School at the turn of the twentieth century. For families not able to take advantage of this opportunity, another generation would pass before the opportunity would present itself again.

The generally accepted number of years social scientists say comprise a generation is usually twenty-five years. This number considers the average time between the birth of the parent and that of their offspring. For school enrollment, add five years to this for the start of elementary school; and another eight for high school entry. This extended time helps in part to explain the slow economic rise of Boston's early Irish immigrants. Although a sizable number of Irish emigrated to the U.S. as early as the 1840s and 1850s, it was not until much later that a meaningful rise in their educational attainment and economic mobility was realized.

LATIN SCHOOL STUDENT ETHNICITY

The changes in the ethnic make-up of Latin School students in the first half of the twentieth century have been examined by some of the school's historians. But none of these studies can provide precise ethnographic data, as school records did not record ethnic origins. To dissect these origins, a study was conducted by the school's newspaper in the 1990s of family names beginning in 1908. It lists thirty-four Sullivans, and twenty-three each of Kelly, Murphy, and Donovan. Names of Jewish descent included Cohen, which appears twenty-eight times and Levine, eleven times. Another analysis of the Class of 1950, conducted by the author, used that year's yearbook information and judgment as to each graduate's likely ethnicity. This retrospective analysis, albeit a bit biased, demonstrates a graduating class comprised of 40 percent

Jewish, 29 percent Irish, 12 percent Italian, 6 percent Greek, and 13 percent "all other." Anglos fell in this last group. The immigrant story perhaps is best told in a story of a historic family of Irish decent, with a deep-rooted Latin School connection.

THE FITZGERALDS AND THE KENNEDYS

In 1987, historian and Pulitzer Prize-winning author Doris Kearns Goodwin, published a 950-page work bearing the title noted above. It began as a turn-of-the-century story of two impoverished Irish immigrant families, both from Boston, and both of whom took steps toward fulfilling the American Dream for themselves and their children. Along their journey, the Latin School was one of these steps, attended by John F. Fitzgerald, class of 1884, and Joseph P. Kennedy, class of 1908.

John F. Fitzgerald, who would become the first Boston-born Irish mayor, was the son of Thomas Fitzgerald, who left Ireland during the potato famine. Fitzgerald started out as a street peddler, then became a shopkeeper, tavern owner, and eventually prosperous landlord. He had three daughters and nine sons. His namesake, born in 1863, was a bright student, and after graduating from the Latin School, was admitted without examination to Harvard Medical School, where half of new entrants already held a bachelor's degree. Unfortunately, he had to withdraw after a year because of the death of his father. To support and hold their large family together, young John would now seek employment.

As pointed out earlier, one of the best upward-mobility opportunities for Irish lads lay in politics. This became the path that young John would pursue—first as a paid assistant to the North End's local ward boss, then as an elected city, and later state official. The most important of these offices, however, was as Boston's mayor, to which John Fitzgerald was elected in 1906. He had campaigned vigorously, using his warmth and natural talents as a politician. He gained the nickname "Honey Fitz," for his "honey-sweet voice," and singing of "Sweet Adeline" at his campaign rallies. Usually accompanying him at the gatherings was his eldest and favorite daughter, Rose, whose name has an indelible place in history books.

At the same time, across the harbor from the North End in East Boston, there was another Irish immigrant family, one headed by P.J. Kennedy. Born in 1858, Kennedy went to work at age fourteen to help support his family of four after his father's death. Hard working and thrifty, he saved enough to buy a tavern, then another, and two more before also becoming a liquor importer. It was in this prosperous family that one of his two sons, Joseph P. Kennedy, was raised. Joseph was sent to the Latin School, where he was class president. He went on to Harvard, where he graduated in 1912.

Two years later, in 1914, the Fitzgeralds and the Kennedys, would become one. On October 7, 1914, Rose Fitzgerald, the twenty-four-year-old daughter of John F. Fitzgerald, was wed to Joseph P. Kennedy, the rising twenty-six-year-old banker, and son of P.J. Kennedy. Historian Doris Kearns Goodwin writes that the wedding was a simple one in the private chapel of William Cardinal O'Connell, and attended by only seventy-five guests.

Later that year, John Fitzgerald, who was mayor at the time of the marriage, was pressured to end his time in elected office. Like many of the city's politicians, charges of patronage and cronyism eventually ended his career. Fitzgerald lived until 1950, long enough to see his namesake and grandson, John Fitzgerald Kennedy, begin a political career of his own in the same North End congressional district. Joseph P. Kennedy, John's father, would live to see his son inaugurated president in 1961. He had his own long and successful career as a banker, liquor importer, and Hollywood film mogul; he also had vast real estate holdings. He also was the first chairman of the Securities and Exchange Commission (SEC), and a pre-World War II ambassador to England. Like many historic figures who preceded the Fitzgeralds and the Kennedys, theirs is one more example of how the American Dream was realized—one in which had Boston Latin School beginnings.

LATIN SCHOOL FACULTY DIVERSITY

By the mid-twentieth century, the ethnic makeup of the Latin School faculty had changed as well. Phillip Marson, a Master at that time, reported that 60 percent of faculty were now of Irish descent, and 14 percent were Jewish. Only one faculty member was Anglo-Saxon.

The first half of the twentieth century also saw the beginnings of a series of non-Anglo Head Masters. Patrick T. Campbell became Head Master in 1920. He had served on the faculty since 1897. He was followed by Joseph L. Powers in 1929, who had joined the faculty in 1906. Powers in turn was followed by George L. McKim, who became Head Master in 1948, and Wilfred O'Leary in 1964. These five consecutive Head Masters during the fifty-year period that began in 1920 were all of Irish descent. In 1977, Michael G. Contompasis, who was of Greek descent, would take over as Head Master and hold that position for the next twenty years.

LATIN SCHOOL GENDER DIVERSITY

In 1877, a petition was submitted to the Boston School Committee calling for the admission of girls to the Latin School. It was rejected, and in its place, steps were taken to open a separate but similar college preparatory secondary school for girls. In February 1878, the Girls' Latin School opened with thirty-seven female students.

It must be remembered that at the time, "separate but equal" was an accepted school standard, whether it applied to Black or white students, or male or female students. Also at the time, college preparatory studies weren't necessarily considered essential for women, whose primary role was still construed to be in the home. Only a handful of universities accepted women as students, and in New England, all-female institutions were just beginning, including Wellesley College in 1875 and Radcliffe in 1879.

No doubt in the minds of Boston school officials, a Girls' Latin School would adequately serve the community's gender diversity needs. For other higher education options, the opening of vocational schools for girls would suffice. In the first decade of the twentieth century, a High School of Practical Arts was opened, a Trade School for Girls, and the Boston Clerical School.

It would be many more years before access would be granted to female students to the all-male Boston Latin School. "Separate but equal" would soon become an obsolete practice and finally end with the school desegregation rulings in the 1950s and 1960s. The feminist movement spurred by the publication of Betty Friedan's book *The Feminine Mystique*, and the founding of the National Organization for Women (NOW) would help to accelerate this change. On the federal legal front, these efforts were furthered by the *Civil Rights Act* of 1964, the Equal Employment Opportunity Commission, the proposed Equal Rights Amendment in 1972, and the Title IX Statute relating to education.

Closer to home, legal actions were underway to bring about female admission to the Latin School. In 1971, a group of female students who had been denied admission to the Girls' Latin School based on their test scores filed a federal civil suit in the Massachusetts District Court. In the complaint, *Bray v. Lee,* the plaintiffs argued that boys with lower test scores were being accepted at Boston Latin, while girls with higher scores were denied entry to Girls' Latin School. The reason for the discrepancy was not intentional, but rather simple mathematics: the fact that the larger Latin School for boys could accommodate twice as many new entrants as Girls' Latin. Because of fewer entry spaces, female admission to a Latin School was more competitive, requiring higher test scores. Citing the Equal Protection Clause of the Fourteenth Amendment, in February of 1972, a judge ruled that, "female students seeking admission to a Boston Latin School have been illegally discriminated against, solely because of their sex, and that discrimination has denied them their constitutional rights to an education equal to that offered to male students."

Eight months later, in September of 1972, the first females entered the doors of the Latin School on Avenue Louis Pasteur. They, like the boys before them, were welcomed in the Assembly Hall by Wilfred O'Leary, the

Head Master, who would now be responsible for the transition of the school to a co-educational institution. As might be expected, the transition would call for modification of the school's physical facilities, its extra-curricular and sports programs and, most importantly, male-female student social interactions. The school compliantly met all these new challenges and held to its long-held principles of equality of opportunity. As one male alumnus sarcastically, but humorously recalled the events of September 1972, "Girls would now be given the opportunity to study as hard as us."

DESEGREGATION AND AFFIRMATIVE ACTION

The 1970s would see other important events that would change the makeup of the Latin School student body. A group of black parents, in conjunction with the National Association for the Advancement of Colored People (NAACP), filed a suit in March of 1972 against the Boston School Committee, charging that the Boston public schools were *de facto* segregated. The federal suit, labeled *Morgan v. Hennigan,* was filed in the U.S. District Court for Massachusetts. The major focus of the suit was the absence of racial balance in Boston elementary and secondary schools, with white students being dominant in those schools in better white neighborhoods, and Black students in poorer neighborhoods where the schools were, they believed, inferior. The plaintiffs in this case claimed that discrimination also existed in faculty hiring and staffing practices, and in the allocation of educational resources for white versus Black schools.

The Boston Latin School was one of three so-called academically selective institutions, or "exam schools," cited in the case. The Girls' Latin and the Boston Technical High School were the other two. The plaintiffs claimed that for these schools the School Committee, "implemented pupil classification practices which discriminate against some children in admission to certain schools." The plaintiffs' arguments were the fact that there were few Blacks enrolled in the more prestigious exam schools. Admission tests were also seen as discriminatory, as they were thought to measure academic achievement rather than aptitude, in which Blacks were believed to traditionally perform

better. Finally, the plaintiffs argued that the exam schools were an insepara-
ble and integral part of a segregated system, and therefore, complicit in its
discrimination practices.

In June of 1974, presiding Judge W. Arthur Garrity, ruled that, "the
Boston School Committee had knowingly carried out a systematic program
of segregation affecting all of the city's students, teachers, and school facul-
ties." The most significant parts of his ruling were that "all schools must reflect
the racial balance of the city's overall student racial balance as a whole," within
an allowable plus or minus 5 percent range. His remedies to eliminate the
alleged segregation practices were to be divided into phases. The first phase,
implemented at the start of the school year in September of 1974, started with
busing 18,000 school children to other neighborhood schools, to achieve the
goal of racial balance in the individual schools.

Boston historians have documented what tragically occurred when the
busing began, including boycotts, riots, and violence that resulted in ston-
ing, firebombing, and shootings. Hundreds of police had to be called upon
to patrol streets and protect both black and white students who were being
bused into each other's neighborhoods. For months thereafter, Boston, once
termed, "the cradle of liberty," was now the scene of racial hatred and conflict.

The second phase of the Garrity rulings began a year later, in September
of 1975, when the exam schools were ordered to change their admissions policies, and now admit 35 percent of their applicants from Black and Hispanic
families. This affirmative action remedy continued under the court order
until November of 1987, and voluntarily thereafter by the School Committee
for another decade. The Latin School would therefore operate for more than
twenty years under these affirmative action admissions requirements. But
the story does not end here.

In the fall of 1997, the 35 percent quota policy came to an end. Its
demise resulted from a pending suit by a white girl's father, whose daughter
had been denied admission to the Latin School, despite scoring higher in the
entrance exams than 103 minority applicants who were admitted under the

35 percent rule. Rather than a court battle, the School Committee voluntarily ended the quota plan, with the intention of replacing it with a more open admission policy, but one that still give some degree of preference to minority applicants. The new plan called for accepting half of applicants based on elementary grades and exam scores; the other half, from top scoring minorities, divided in proportion to their representation in the applicant pool.

The new 50/50 plan was a short-lived one. Michael C. McLaughlin, the attorney father in the 1997 case, also challenged this plan on behalf of his new client, Henry Wessman, whose white daughter was denied admission to the Latin School. In November 1998, a three-judge panel struck down the 50/50 plan. Affirmative action policies by the School Committee, the exam schools, and the Latin School, came to an end.

What is most significant about this tumultuous twenty-three-year period in the Latin School's history is how the school successfully handled the changes required in its admissions policy, and how it maintained its standards of excellence, while helping a new influx of minorities accomplish what generations before them had achieved. They too could pass through this gateway of opportunity.

In the first year of affirmative action, from 1975 to 1976, Wilfred L. O'Leary had been Head Master for ten years prior to the Garrity rulings. For the next twenty-one years, and his entire term during the affirmative action period, Michael G. Contompasis was the school's Head Master.

The son of Greek immigrant parents, Contompasis grew up in a modest three-story home in the Roslindale section of Boston. Like many other first-generation children, he and his parents saw the Latin School as a gateway to opportunity. He enrolled in the school and graduated in the Class of 1957. After college, he taught science in two of the city's high schools, before becoming a Master at the Latin School. In 1977, he was appointed its Head Master. It would be on his shoulders that the primary responsibility for managing the affirmative action transition would fall. As we saw for other Memorable Masters during the school's history, this Master would rise to the enormous challenge that desegregation and affirmative action brought with them.

The Head Master and the faculty at the Latin School wanted to make minority acceptance work, elevating the educational skills of the new groups, and not lowering the school's standards, or diluting its curriculum. Many years later, in an interview for this book, Head Master Contompasis recalled the challenge that he and his colleagues faced, and what they thought was really necessary to make affirmative action work. He saw the task as calling for much more than a few superficial changes. Rather, he said:

> What was necessary was a change in the culture of the school—creating a different kind of atmosphere, one which would give these new students every possible opportunity to succeed—even though initially many may not have the same kind of strong foundations that entering students had in the past.

The Head Master's strong convictions and commitment to his pupils is evident in interviews conducted among alumni who attended the school during these transition years. Charmane Higgins, a black female student from the Class of 1987, who later was recognized as a Distinguished Graduate, spoke of him as, "a father figure, with a deep sense of responsibility for all of us." Following his retirement, and a later position as Boston's Superintendent of Schools, his friends and alumni set up a website on which those who knew him could pay tribute. Over 100 grateful tributes to his leadership were posted on the site.

To accomplish the new goals set by the school over the next several years, several student support programs were introduced to boost the academic performance of the school's new pupils and reduce the likelihood of dropouts. Most of those support programs continue today. Under the director of the newly created McCarthy Institute for Transition and Support, a Saturday Success School program was established. Alumni volunteers provided individual remedial instruction to students for up to three hours each Saturday during the academic year. After-school tutoring was also made available, with academic assistance available to students in Classes VI, V, and IV on a walk-in basis during after-school hours. Tutors were drawn from the three senior classes of students. Peer tutoring by Class I seniors was also available during study periods. Finally, the number of guidance counselors was increased, and their responsibilities redefined. In earlier years, counseling was largely limited to advising students on college choices and their entrance requirements. More focus would now be given to helping students who may be having difficulty with their study habits and grade performance.

With new support programs in place, the last quarter of the twentieth century marked the end of the "sink or swim" philosophy that characterized the Latin School for so many years. No longer would Head Masters give the legendary Assembly Hall welcome to entering Class VI students: "Look to your left, look to your right; the person you are looking at may not be here six years from now."

Beyond these in-school support activities, the school initiated an ambitious outreach program directed at parents of prospective minority applicants, ethnic community organizations, and elementary schools from which applicants would be drawn. Latin School representatives visited these feeder schools and recruited high-performing students and introduced the pupils and their parents to the Latin School. The visits included an offer for a free summer program to prepare prospective applicants for the school's next entrance exam.

During the early years of the affirmative action ruling, the federal court carefully monitored the school's progress in meeting the goals that had been set by its rulings. This oversight took the form of compliance meetings, with the Head Master called upon, for example, to explain student dropout situations, and reasons why a dropout occurred. The school received much pro bono assistance in these sessions from attorney William F. Looney, Jr., a 1949 Latin School alumnus.

For those involved in these difficult years, there was the belief that if the school did not make affirmative action work, it ran the risk of seeing its long life come to an end. Many might have argued for its closing, characterizing it as a dated, elite institution for whites only—out of sync with the new and different multicultural city that Boston was becoming. By 1980, a third of the city's population was non-white; at the time the affirmative action program ended, it had risen to 40 percent.

Symbolic of the changes that occurred in these transition years was an event that occurred in 1985, upon the tenth anniversary of the start of the affirmative action, and the Latin School's 350th anniversary. Invited to give the keynote address at the ceremonies was a distinguished Black alumnus, Clifford R. Wharton, Jr. In his Class of 1943, he was one of only three Black students. He went on to Harvard and earned advanced degrees at John Hopkins University and the University of Chicago. After a long and successful career in international economic development, and the first Black CEO of a Fortune 500 company, he became president of Michigan State University. Aside from his selection to speak at one of the school's most historic events, his remarks that day were also significant as he made no mention of his color. He was just another Latin School graduate who had made good.

NEW ASIAN-AMERICAN STUDENT DIVERSITY

Hidden beneath the African American and Hispanic school issues that characterized the 1974-1998 period was another set of circumstances that would change the ethnic makeup of the Latin School student body. In 1965, U.S. immigration laws were changed, opening the doors of our country to prospective immigrants from Asia. Since the turn of the twentieth century, immigration law was based on historic quotas that favored European immigrants. Earlier in the history of the Latin School, it was the offspring of these European immigrants who, for the first time, changed the ethnic makeup of the Latin School student body.

Between 1970 and 2000, a third of all U.S. immigrant arrivals were from Asian countries—largely from China, the Philippines, India, Korea, and Vietnam. The Asian-American population of Boston grew from less than 10,000 in 1970 to almost 50,000 by the year 2000. As the city's

Asian-American population grew, so did its proportion of Latin School enrollments—reaching 28 percent of total enrollment in 2010. What's significant is that Asian-Americans represented only 9 percent of the city's population. Asian-Americans were therefore more than three times as likely to become Latin School students as those from the city's population.

Why the high achievement for this group? In 2012, the highly respected Pew Research Center conducted an extensive survey of Asian-Americans on values and attributes relating to their families and children. What emerged from the study is the importance placed on parenthood, hard work, and career success for themselves and their offspring. Measured against the U.S. population, ratings on the importance of these values were significantly higher—in some cases double the all-population averages. These findings are consistent with those of other studies, and data relating to educational and career achievements levels for Asian-Americans. These factors are no doubt contributing factors to the higher and disproportionate enrollment levels for this minority group at the Latin School and other such schools. In New York City, half or more of the enrollment of the prestigious Stuyvesant High School and Bronx High School of Science are Asian-Americans.

Turn-of-the-century immigration clearly changed the ethnic composition of the Latin School student body—with the sons of these immigrants taking advantage of the school's role as a gateway of opportunity for realizing the American Dream. Personal stories of such alumni as the Fitzgeralds and the Kennedys help us understand that dream of upward mobility. As the student body continued to change from period to period, the Latin School's core values did not. Its high standards of performance, classical-based curriculum, rigorous study, and disciplinary requirements were never compromised.

The second half of the twentieth century also saw changes, but again, the school would adjust to them, and in the end come out stronger because of them. Females were admitted in 1972. The desegregation and school busing crisis came in 1974, and with it a two-decade period in which Latin School admission requirements were mandated by affirmative action rulings. The school can be proud of how it handled these changes. It held to its deep-rooted conviction that the school would provide equal opportunity for all.

The Latin School had become a multicultural institution, with significantly more racial and ethnic diversity than in the past. If one stands outside the school's doorway at day-end dismissal time today, there is truly a heartwarming American experience to behold: students, male and female, of all races and ethnic origin, leaving the school with book-laden backpacks, playfully jostling with one another. As one faculty member put it, "They may be of different colors on the outside, but on the inside, they are all purple"— purple being the school color.

CHAPTER VII:

Academic Depth and Excellence

No man reached to excellence in any one art or profession without having passed through the slow and painful process of study and preparation.

—HORACE MANN

LATIN SCHOOL LESSONS OF THE past can tell us a lot about the factors that have contributed to the school's success, both in terms of its academic programs, and its ability to instill lifelong virtues and values in its students. Much of the success of the Latin School can be traced back to its classical education lessons of yesterday that have been blended with the contemporary needs of today's students.

From the very beginning of the Latin School, the curriculum set forth was patterned after English grammar schools. The roots of those institutions can be traced all the way back to the ancient Greek and Roman practices in educating young people. The educators of that time termed these concepts, and what continued for several hundred years thereafter, as *classical education.*

In Greek society dating back to 600 B.C., boys aged seven to fourteen attended schools where they received both mental and physical training. Here they learned their three Rs: *Rding, Rting* and *Rthmatic.* Their physical training encompassed running, jumping, discus, and javelin throwing. There was always a clear understanding that both the minds and bodies of their young citizens should be developed if they were to participate in the cultural and civic life of the city-state in a meaningful way. The schools were called *gymnasiums.* It was within this environment that the famous Greek sophists and philosophers, including Aristotle and Plato, gained notoriety with their lessons in reasoning, logic, and the importance of morality and virtues. They saw education in its larger context. Not narrow training in occupational skills, but rather the development of broadly educated, well-rounded, and highly reasoning individuals.

Macedonia, one of the early Greek-city states, survived until 143 B.C., when it was conquered by the Romans. Respectful of the Greek culture, the Romans continued much of what the Greeks had established in the principles of a classical education. Formal education began for individuals at seven years of age and learnings included how to read both Latin and Greek. This was followed by what the Romans called *Grammaticus,* which included the study of grammar, sentence structure, and syntax. This was then supplemented by readings of Latin writers. Where the Greeks studied Homer, the Romans studied their own countryman, Virgil, a poet who is best known for his national epic, the Aeneid, a work honoring Rome and predicting the rise of its empire.

The Grecian and Roman classical education concepts became the standards on which the lycées and gymnasium schools on the European continent were later modeled, as were the English grammar schools. What these schools all had in common was that they were language-based, rigorous, and demanding. They encompassed respect for studying and learning from the wisdom of great thinkers of the past. There was also a strict student discipline embedded in these learnings, with swift and often stern punishment for infractions. Memorization, drills, repetition, and recitation were important learning tools. The teacher was the Master, with absolute and arbitrary authority over the classroom. The Master usually stood on a raised platform and was always addressed in a formal manner. The curriculum was based on the *trivium* subjects of grammar, logic, and rhetoric. While subject matter content was important by itself, the way it was taught and learned always had broader objectives: to encourage learning, to train the mind, and to enhance one's reasoning and critical-thinking abilities. If we were to define a classical education, it would be as follows: a traditional and enduring form of education begun by the ancient Greeks and Romans, with emphasis on language, logic, and rhetoric. Usually rigorous, demanding, and disciplined, it makes use of memorization, drills, repetition, and recitation to develop the students' learning skills and character. The core curriculum is generally uniform and mandatory, with focus on preparing the student for higher education, rather than for a commercial or vocational occupation.

THE STUDY OF LATIN

It may come as a surprise that the study of Latin continues today in so many schools. Although thought to be a dead language by some, it is very much alive. Nationally, the *New York Times* reported that 135,000 students take the College Board National Latin exam, up by a third since 1998. The rationale for the study of Latin in the past still holds true today. Over half of the English vocabulary is derived from Latin. The English principles of grammar are all based on the Latin language—nouns, plurals, verbs, prepositions, tenses, prefixes, and suffixes. Latin therefore helps students understand grammar and build their vocabulary. The language also lays the foundation for the study of other Latin-based languages—the so-called Romance languages including Spanish, French, Portuguese, Italian, and Romanian. Latin is also the language base for legal terms, for example, *corpus delecti* (concrete evidence), *habeas corpus* (protection against unlawful and indefinite imprisonment), and *nolo contendere* (no contest). The same holds true for many medical and pharmaceutical terms including *recipere* (Rx, or prescription) and *bis in die* *(bid, or twice a day)*.

The process of learning the Latin language brings with it other important educational benefits by virtue of its structure, discipline, and attention to detail. As one educational expert has put it, "Every lesson in Latin is a lesson in logic." Some of the same benefits can be found in the study of ancient Greek, from which a third of English words are derived. For those who have studied Latin and Greek in their school years, they will tell you that, though they would not be able to translate a line of the languages today, what has stayed with them are the learning disciplines that their study of them provided.

CLASSICAL EDUCATION CRITICISM

Though classical education remained the standard for educational excellence for so many years, criticism began to emerge in the late nineteenth century. Led by John Dewey, and others, reform was set forth that became known as the *progressive education movement.* The basic premise of this movement was that a classical education was too narrow and restricted in meeting the needs of citizens in a new industrial society. It wasn't considered practical enough and did not prepare students for the growing number of commercial and vocational jobs that were now needed in a burgeoning economy.

Progressive education proponents argued not only for a broader-based curriculum, but also for changes in the way students were taught in the classroom. Rote learning through memorization, drill, and repetition was criticized. It would inhibit creativity. They saw the all-powerful and dominant role of the teacher as an anachronism. Many felt that teachers should be more facilitators than lecturers and disciplinarians. More classroom discussion should occur and replace individual recitations.

The counter argument to this movement was that a progressive path would result in a lowering of educational performance standards, and that it is much too permissive. Traditional classical education worked for hundreds of years, producing educated citizens who became leaders in science, business, and the arts.

The classical versus progressive debate continued. Like all polar points of view, the answer may be somewhere in the middle. It doesn't have to be an "either/or" case, where a single educational philosophy should prevail. College may not be for everyone. The Boston School Committee understood this when in 1822, it established a non-classical school, the Boston English High School. It stood side-by-side with the Latin School, serving different student needs. Later, Boston opened a technical high school and a high school of commerce. A similar model exists in Germany where the Federal Ministry of Education oversees work-study apprentice programs that offer training in 350 different occupations. Almost half of Germany's young people are enrolled in the occupational-oriented programs. For others who wish to pursue alternate paths, college preparatory programs exist.

THE COTTON CURRICULUM

The Latin School curriculum has always been characterized by a high degree of continuity over the course of the school's history. The original curriculum, thought to be largely the doings of John Cotton, remained essentially unchanged for almost 250 years. Cotton had patterned it after that of the English grammar schools.

Not until the 1870s were there any significant changes in the Cotton curriculum. As noted earlier, these changes were largely influenced by Charles William Eliot, a Latin School and Harvard graduate who, as one of the nation's leading educators, served as Harvard president for forty-one years. Eliot was consulted regularly on education matters by Boston's civic leaders. Also, in his position at Harvard, he had a strong influence on college preparatory school studies by setting college entrance requirements. As a long-time educational leader and spokesman for the National Education Association (NEA), his importance was felt for many years by public school educators throughout the country.

The changes he brought to the Latin School academic curriculum were an increased emphasis on English grammar, composition, and literature. Science and history were given more attention, as were modern, as opposed to classical languages. French was added to the curriculum in 1852 followed by German in 1874. The modern but important changes that began in the 1870s lasted through the first half of the twentieth century. In the science curriculum, physics was added in 1880. Chemistry wasn't added until 1933. Today, the Latin school continues to require four years of study of a modern language, including Chinese, French, German, Italian, or Spanish. Apropos of the school's name, four years of Latin is also required for students entering grade seven, and three years for students entering in grade nine.

Throughout the years, the Latin School's curriculum was a demanding one, with students expected to master their subject matter and perform with high standards of excellence. Noted historian Doris Kearns Goodwin in her book *The Fitzgeralds and The Kennedys* uncovered an 1884 Latin School examination that the young John Fitzgerald would have taken. It demonstrates the rigorous nature of the curriculum, and what was expected of the students. The exam included some of the following:

- Latin: Translate Cicero and Virgil at sight and explain its symbolism.

- History: Describe the forms of government and the classes in which people were divided in the Heroic Age. Explain the causes of Peloponnesian War.

- English: Write an account of Mark Antony in Shakespeare's Forum scene. Explain Milton's role as a poet.

- Mathematics: Solve a series of algebra and geometry problems.

- Physics: Illustrate the laws of attraction and repulsion between currents of electricity.

Interviews with alumni are replete with stories and recollections of rigorous exams, including their scope, depth, and severity. And the examination process was not one that only occurred at a marking period's end. It was a daily and weekly process. Daily, there were class recitations in which a random student might be called upon to translate a Latin passage, given as part of the prior night's homework assignment. Students were graded on their recitation. Perhaps it would be two days in a row, or not at all. Students were called upon by their last name. They then stood up and faced the Master. If he were to be addressed, it was always as "Yes, sir" or "No, sir." One learned quickly not to try to predict whom the Master would call upon. Weekly tests on the subject matter followed, and then a monthly report card, to be brought home and signed by a parent.

The monthly grading system was as precise as the standards expected of the students: not an easy *pass/fail* grade, not a *letter* grade. For many years, it was a specific numeric grade, not in simple five-or-ten-point increments, but much more precise: 64 percent, 82 percent, etc. A passing grade was 60 percent. Anything below this was considered to be a failing grade, and was recorded boldly in red ink on one's summary record card—the permanent school record kept in the Head Master's office. In so many instances, these small but important grading subtleties worked to shape the unique character of the school's academic standards.

CONTEMPORARY CLASSICAL EDUCATION

The current Latin School mission statement sets forth the goals of the school in the following words:

> Boston Latin School seeks to ground its students in a contemporary classical education as preparation for successful college studies, responsible and engaged citizenship, and a rewarding life.

The statement goes on to elaborate why these goals are important, and how the school helps its students accomplish them. It was prepared under the direction School Head Cornelia Kelley and reflects her strong belief in educating the "whole person." She quotes the Latin *mens sana in corpora sano,* meaning, "a sound mind in a sound body," as a guiding principle. The descriptive *contemporary classical,* used for the first time in 2005, will likely continue in the future. It recognizes that, while the school continues its adherence to the principles and traditions of a classical education, it has made modifications in the school's curriculum to meet the modern, contemporary needs of its students. This is evidenced by its unchanged language-based curriculum; its belief in the importance of the *trivium*—grammar, logic, and rhetoric; its respect for the importance of the wisdom of the past; its rigorous, demanding curriculum and stern disciplinary practices; and its goal of building character in its students.

The curriculum changes that have been made start with far more emphasis on science and mathematics—reflecting the school's understanding that we live in a world today where the knowledge of science, technology, engineering, and mathematics—the so-called STEM (short for science, technology, engineering, and math) disciplines have become more important than ever before. Greater emphasis and a broader choice in the study of modern languages have been made, reflecting the fact that the world is now without borders, as globalization of commercial and cultural life is occurring all around us.

As our society has changed and become more diverse both demographically and in terms of cultural interests, individuality has grown in importance. Our young people want more avenues of self-expression for their individual needs and interests. Recognizing this, the Latin School curriculum has been broadened, with more electives open to students—and more opportunities for pursuing individual interests.

SCHOOL ENTRANCE REQUIREMENTS

The school's entrance requirements continue to be stringent, based on the acceptance of students who demonstrate the potential for educational excellence. Students may enter the school at the seventh-grade level (Class VI), or ninth-grade level (Class IV). One must be a resident of the City of Boston itself or the thirteen other neighborhood towns that are part of the city. Acceptance is competitive, based on the school's assessment of the prospective student's elementary school academic record, and scores of written entrance examinations.

A multiple-choice test is given to all applicants, using the Independent Schools Entrance Exam (ISEE), prepared, and administered by an outside organization, like the College Board. The exam is in three parts: (1) a verbal and quantitative reading test that measures a student's capability for learning; (2) a reading comprehension and math achievement test, to measure strengths and weaknesses in these areas; and (3) a written essay—not graded but available to the school if it wants to review it. Scores for the first two tests are reported to the school on a scaled, percentile basis, tied to average national scores reported for all students taking the tests over the prior three-year period.

Applications, along with the student's elementary school record and ISEE test scores are then reviewed by the school. Equal weight is given to one's elementary school record and test scores to calculate a composite score. In terms of acceptance levels, approximately 400 candidates are usually invited to enter the Latin School Class VI; another fifty to seventy-five, Class IV. The acceptance rate is estimated to be a third of those expressing an interest in the school.

TWENTY-FIRST CENTURY CURRICULUM

The Latin School academic program is now organized into eight departments, each headed by a Program Director.

- English
- Mathematics
- Science
- History
- Classics
- Modern Languages
- Visual and Performing Arts
- Physical Education

The school year course load consists of five full-year courses in Classes VI and V, and six full-year courses in Classes IV to I, some of which are mandatory, and others elective. For graduation, four years are required of English, mathematics, and a foreign language. For six-year students, four years of Latin are also a requirement; three years for four-year students. Laboratory science is mandatory for three years.

The school's curriculum also includes an Advanced Placement program, with a total of twenty-four courses taught in six of the eight academic departments. This represents almost one quarter of the school's total course offerings. Prerequisites are set for these courses. The standards and course content are established in a syllabus developed by the College Board. The Board also administers an examination for each course. Scores are reported to the Latin School and to colleges designated by the students, where they are seeking entrance and college credits.

Each college determines on its own the credits it gives to the student applicant. The individual academic departments in the Latin School provide detailed summaries of the objectives and content of each of their course offerings. Highlights of these follows.

English

The English Department believes that it has an important obligation to provide students with a solid foundation in reading and writing. It is for this reason that entering Class VI students are required to take two full-year English courses, both in the same year—one in reading, one in writing. These students then go on to Class V, with a requirement for a third course in English language arts. These three foundation courses encompass grammar, syntax, vocabulary building, and composition. There is also an introduction to American and world literature through the reading and study of nonfiction, fiction, and other literary forms. And outside and summer reading is assigned to instill good reading habits in the school's students.

For those entering the school in Class VI, there will still be four more years of English courses—a requirement for graduation. For students entering in Class IV, each of their four years carries a requirement for an English course. Declamation is also a mandatory requirement in Class VI through Class III English. Each student must give three classroom presentations each year, on which they are graded. Finally, the English Department curriculum includes two AP courses in language and composition.

The end and broader goals of the school's English curriculum are to "develop analytical readers, creative writers, articulate speakers, attentive listeners, critical thinkers, and disciplined researchers."

Mathematics

Historically, mathematics has been an important part of the school's curriculum, and this has been continued but on an expanded basis, with both basic and upper-level courses. The department has ten courses in all, as well as four college-level Advanced Placement ones. The courses cover algebra, geometry, trigonometry, and calculus. There is also a statistics course elective for those having completed math requirements through pre-calculus. Among the four Advanced Placement courses are a computer science and a college-level statistics course.

Science

The science curriculum encompasses four disciplines: biology, chemistry, physics, and earth science. There are eight courses in all, with both basic and upper-level courses in biology, chemistry, and physics.

Class VI students are required to take the earth science course familiarizing them with the individual disciplines of astronomy, oceanography, meteorology, and geology. Biology is a requirement for all Class IV students. Chemistry and physics are electives, open to students in Classes III, II, and I. Since three full years of high school-level sciences are required for graduation, the curriculum for these Class IV to Class I students reflects the significant importance of science in their overall study program. All the science courses include a laboratory component. During 1988-89, when the school building underwent renovations, new science and computer labs were constructed. The science curriculum also offers four Advanced Placement courses—in biology, chemistry, physics, and environmental science. When the mathematics and science curricula are looked at together, their scope and depth are now impressive, and address the growing need in our society for better levels of education in these disciplines. In total, the two departments offer twenty-six courses in all, eight of which are in the Advanced Placement category. These science and math courses now represent the equivalent of one quarter of all the courses offered by the school.

History

This department's courses encompass U.S. history and government, world history, art history and economics—with a total of thirteen courses, four of which are Advanced Placement.

One U.S. history course is required for graduation, with a mandatory requirement that a basic course be taken in Class II. The course covers the period through the Civil War and Reconstruction. There is also a second course starting with Reconstruction through to the present. For those more interested in our country's history, there are two elective courses—American Government and Colonial Foreign Policy.

World history is taught in two courses, both required for graduation. They are divided into chronological periods. The first course required is in Class IV. In addition to the study of the history of major regions of the world, students gain an insight into the world's different cultures and religions— Buddhism, Hinduism, Judaism, Christianity, and Islam. The second course, required in Class III, includes a study of the Renaissance, the Reformation, the Enlightenment, and the Industrial Revolution.

As in other departments, Advanced Placement courses are offered— American Government, Economics, and Modern European history.

Classics

Courses in Latin and Greek are the responsibility of the Classics Department. Four levels of Latin language courses are offered, two of which have a broader language/cultural perspective, and one upper-level course involving Latin prose and poetry. For six-year students at the school, four years of Latin are required; for four-year students, three years. The study of ancient Greek, which was once mandatory, now is limited to two elective courses, available to Class II and Class I students.

The Latin School's movement from pure classical education to contemporary classical is clearly seen in the reduced number of classical language course offerings, relative to that offered by other departments in the school. With just eleven courses, they now represent only 10 percent of the school's more than 100 courses. And only one of the twenty-four Advanced Placement offerings is now in the classics.

Modern Languages

It was only in the late nineteenth century that French and then German was added to the school's curriculum. And then, for close to a century, they were the only modern language choices open to students. That has now changed, with Spanish, Italian, and Chinese added to the curriculum.

For each language there is a four-year ladder, from the basic course through upper-level courses. Four years of one foreign language are required for graduation, taken during any year from Class V to Class I. Advanced Placement courses are available for each of the five languages. The fact that there are four years of study available in any given modern language gives a student the opportunity to become fluent in that language. And, through readings in the language, the student also gains an understanding of the language's literature, culture, and customs.

Visual and Performing Arts

During the period 1999-2002, the Latin School underwent a major building renovation and expansion. It included a totally new building, with both classrooms and special facilities specifically designed for the study of art and music. The new facilities then became the basis for expansion of the school's art and music studies in four categories—drama, instrumental music, vocal music, and the visual arts. The latter includes painting, drawing, sculpture, photography, graphic design, and digital art. In the above categories, a total of fourteen elective courses are offered to students. School tallies show more than half of students participate in the arts program, either through formal courses during class hours or after school as an extracurricular activity.

The visual and performing arts facilities, courses, and programs offer students unique opportunities to pursue the special interests they might have, to express their individuality and creativity. A more extended discussion of the department's program is included in Chapter IX.

The Humanities

There are several of courses that are included in the English, history, and classical study listings that are worth noting here, as they each possess character-building values for students.

The English Department has a course listed as Humanities I, which is described as a course that "uses art, film, literature, history, and philosophy to explore what it means to be human as well as humane." The History Department has a course titled *Facing History and Ourselves*. It traces the history of discrimination and prejudice throughout history. Its objective is "to equip students to become critically minded citizens, with the ability to think through the big moral and political choices that they will confront as citizens in modern day society." The Classics Department has a course titled *The Myth Tradition*, which examines Greek, Roman, Near Eastern, and Biblical mythology, with life lessons learned from their myths.

The above represent examples of how the school uses its curriculum to take students well beyond a rote knowledge of academic subjects, to stimulate their thinking and reasoning ability, and to help build character.

If one were to summarize the strengths of the Latin School's contemporary classical curriculum, several points would be made. First, it has breadth, with eight academic subject areas and more than 100 courses that include Advanced Placement courses in each. Second, it makes mandatory, important foundation courses—essential for every student's education, regardless of any special interests the student may have. And third, the curriculum has depth; it digs much deeper into the subject matter than traditional survey courses. In most every subject area, students can go on to an additional second, third, or fourth year of study, deepening their knowledge of subjects in which they have particular interest. And finally in the curriculum, there is a balance between required and elective courses, with the academic standards and expectations for the electives as high as those for required courses.

Beyond the subject matter taught in each of the course offerings, Latin School students also learn critical thinking skills. These are acquired through the teaching methods used by the school's faculty. These are the principles of Socratic thinking that focus on giving students questions, not answers, and calls for them to think and reason logically. This begins with the ability to focus, comprehend, and retain information; to analyze, synthesize, and prioritize; and to deal with the abstract and the hypothetical. These are all skills that when learned in the classroom, will last through one's lifetime— well beyond any course subject matter.

Academic Grades

Student academic performance are carefully monitored by the Masters and the school. Report cards, which date back to the early nineteenth century, are issued, reporting grades in each subject. There are five marking periods during the academic year, each averaging two months in length. Signed report cards by parents must be returned to homeroom faculty members. The last report card, issued in June, and containing final year-end grades, is mailed directly to the parent.

To be promoted to the next highest grade, students must pass a minimum of five major subjects (four for Class VI and Class V). If one major subject is failed, the student must attend summer school and pass a makeup exam to remove the failure. For students passing only four major subjects, summer school and passing a makeup exam is mandatory for promotion. Those students passing fewer than four major subjects (three for Class VI and Class V) must repeat the year. If the student chooses to transfer to another school, rather than repeat the year, he/she may attend summer school to gain course credit for the transfer.

Academic Recognition

A long-established practice of the Latin School has been to issue an Approbation Card to students whose grades excel during a given marking period. No grade average lower than 90-92, and 93-96 in conduct earns *Approbation with Distinction;* for those with no grade lower than 80-82, including conduct, a regular *Approbation Card* is issued.

The most significant recognition of student academic performance is in the awarding of prizes and medals. In total there are more than sixty award categories with a third of these for academic excellence. Other awards, to be discussed later, are for special abilities and talent, and qualities of character. The practice of awards dates to 1791, when Benjamin Franklin left 100 pounds sterling for the Boston public schools. Awarded each year on graduation day, Franklin medals are given to the school's top scholars.

Prize winners are usually announced at year-end ceremonies attended by their parents. In his autobiography entitled, *A Passion to Win*, Sumner Redstone, Latin School class of 1940, fondly recounts the evening of his graduation ceremony. Sumner finished first in his class and was to be awarded the Franklin Medal College Scholarship and the classic and modern prizes for his sixth consecutive year. "With my proud parents in the auditorium, I was called to the stage again, again, and again," he said. Redstone later went on to found and lead the nation's largest media and entertainment conglomerate, ViacomCBS, whose holdings includes Paramount, CBS, Nickelodeon, MTV, and other popular cable networks.

For more than 350 years of its history, the Latin School closely followed the principles inherent in a traditional classical education. The record of the school and its graduates is a testament to these strengths. In the latter part of the twentieth century, what was becoming evident, however, is that we were now in a new age—one of scientific breakthroughs, globalization, and changing cultural values. The composition of the Latin School student body was also changing, particularly its gender, racial, and ethnic makeup.

With these transformations, the educational needs of our young people were also changing.

When change occurs in any field, it is important that it be disciplined and orderly. The goals should be to preserve the best of the past, while purposefully adding new elements to its basic structure. This is what the Latin School did—preserving the strengths of its classical education, its language-based curriculum, academic disciplines, and its demanding student workload. The current curriculum, which has been described as *contemporary classical,* reflects these principles. Of the major high-school-level subjects required for graduation, half are still language-based (i.e., courses in English, Latin, and modern languages). Society's growing need for more math and science education is reflected in the fact that a full one-third of the school's graduation requirements are in these course disciplines. The number of electives has also been increased dramatically. And the addition of a Visual and Performing Arts Program, with its fourteen courses, has expanded even further the number of elective choices, as well as opened important areas of study that were not available to students in the past. As a final point, the content of the curriculum, and the disciplines built into it, continue to provide students with strong lessons of character.

CHAPTER VIII:

Lifelong Virtues and Values

The prosperity of a country depends not on the abundance of its resources nor the strength of its fortifications nor the beauty of its public buildings. It consists is in the number of its cultivated citizens, its men of education, enlightenment, and character.

—MARTIN LUTHER

THE LATIN SCHOOL CAN BE proud of the fact that, along with its record of academic excellence, it has also been successful in instilling important lifelong virtues and values in its graduates. In alumni interviews conducted for this book, it was the lessons of character that were cited spontaneously, and most often, in people's recollections of their Latin School experience. The academic courses taken may have been long forgotten, but not the virtues and values that these students came away with—ones they said influenced their lives so much, and for so long after graduation.

The term *virtue* comes from the ancient Greek work *avate*, meaning moral excellence. It is an admirable, desirable, positive quality or trait, one that is usually firmly entrenched in an individual's character. Virtues include such traits as honesty, courage, diligence, and compassion. The term *value*, as used here, relates to the core beliefs, ideals, and attitudes of an individual or group. In some respects, virtues and values are synonymous, but not in all cases. For example, a belief that monetary gain measures one's success may be an important value for some, but not necessarily an admirable one that would make it a virtue.

The teaching of virtues and values to young people goes back more than 2,500 years to the days of Confucius in the East, as well as the ancient Greeks in the West. The lessons of Confucius centered around how the ideal man should live one's life. The likes of Aristotle and Plato did the same for their young people, though with a different method of instruction. This can be seen in Plato's dialogues, where Socrates asks his students to explain a particular virtue. Back-and-forth discourse follows on the different dimensions of the virtue: why it is important, and how it should be practiced in everyday life.

Latin School pupils were familiar with these kinds of philosophical debates through their readings of morality lessons in such works as Aesop's Fables. Simple and homespun, these writings were read by the school's students throughout the seventeenth and eighteenth centuries. All during the colonial period, Puritan morality lessons were also an important part of every child's education. And, Latin School's own Ben Franklin, left us with his list of thirteen virtues, which he said in his autobiography, he tried to live by.

One of the more memorable and often quoted stories that link virtues and values to one's education is that of England's Duke of Wellington, supposedly told upon his homecoming after defeating Napoleon at Waterloo. On his return, he visited Eton, where he had studied as a young boy. Walking through the quadrangle at the school, he reportedly said, "Here is where I learned the lessons that made it possible for me to conquer at Waterloo." Phillips Brooks, an eminent Latin School alumnus, spoke of Wellington at the dedication of the new Warren Street Latin School building in February of 1881.

It was not what he had read there in books, not what he had learned there by writing Greek verses, or by scanning the lines of Virgil and Horace, that helped him win his great battle; but there had had learned to be faithful to present duty, to be strong, to be diligent, to be patient; and that was why he was able to say, that it was what he had learned at Eton that had made it possible for him to conquer at Waterloo.

Brooks went on then to liken the lessons of Eton with those of the Latin School.

CONTINUITY IS KEY

Before examining the virtues and values the Latin School instills in its students, it may be worthwhile to have more context of what the core values are for the school itself. Over the course of its history, the school has been built on several important principles.

THE IMPORTANCE OF TRADITION

It is hard not to experience a strong set of emotions when one remembers, for example, as a young boy of eleven years of age, walking up to the imposing entrance of the Latin School. Four classic columns stand three stories high at the entrance. The heavy double doors are opened, and one walks up a short marble staircase. Built in 1922, the marble flooring is now badly in need of repair, but renovations would only hide the nostalgia associated with knowing that thousands of footsteps have preceded your own.

Facing the entranceway is a statue, sculpted in 1871 by Latin School graduate Richard Saltonstall Greenough. It is "Alma Mater," with a gracious lady crowning her heroes who served in the Civil War. Those alumni who died in the war are named on a shield which she is holding; those who returned are named on two marble tables near the statue.

The next stop is the Assembly Hall, where newly enrolled students traditionally gather to be welcomed by the Head Master. What every new student report noticing and remembering most is the upper frieze of the hall where there are the embossed names of the school's most prominent pupils. Their names are familiar to these newcomers. For every student, the names, and what they stood for, are an integral part of the school's tradition.

Institutions built on tradition like those of the Latin School are truly inspirational. Knowing that you are attending the same school as some of the nation's Founding Fathers is nothing short of awesome. For minority students to know that it was these Latin School graduates who led the abolitionist and racial equity movements in the nineteenth century must carry even greater meaning and relevance. And, to know that you are sitting in the same auditorium that Leonard Bernstein once did makes you think about what similar success for you might someday be, with a career in music and the arts. Tradition gives us an understanding and respect for the past, and for those who lived it.

The 1922 school building, now a century old, is still the symbolic heart and soul of the school. Additions were made in 1932, doubling its original size. In 1988, there was a more complete renovation and extension of the gymnasium and athletic facilities, as well as the addition of computer and science lab classrooms. In 1999, over a three-year period, a new and enlarged library was built, as well as an arts and music complex.

Important in preserving the school's traditions is the Boston Latin School Association, an alumni organization founded in 1844. It has a full-time staff that assists in planning of class reunions and organizing and managing alumni fundraising drives. It also maintains an archive of important historical materials for the school. These activities are unique for a public school, and work to preserve the traditions of the Latin School.

The importance of tradition was the subject of a letter sent on the occasion of the Latin School's 300th anniversary by philosopher and eminent Latin School graduate George Santayana and read at the school's tercentenary ceremonies. With his worldly insight, he wrote, "This fidelity to tradition, I am confident has, and will have its reward. The oldest forms of life, barring accidents, have the longest future."

EQUALITY OF OPPORTUNITY

The virtues and values that our nation was built on are expressed in a few brief, but memorable words in our Declaration of Independence—that "All men are created equal." Based largely on the thinking of seventeenth-century English philosopher John Locke, these are not state-granted rights, but God-given ones in which royalty, nobility, and heredity have no place. As Locke states, "Men being…by nature all free, equal, and independent, no one can be put out of this estate…without his own consent."

From its founding in 1635, as a free and public school open to everyone, the Latin School has been an embodiment of this equality of opportunity ideal. It welcomed the children of colonists from every economic class. Later, with new immigrant arrivals, children from every new ethnic group were welcomed. Theodore H. White, Class of 1932, a political writer, and Pulitzer Prize winner, wrote in his biography that, "The school accepted students without discrimination, and it flunked them—Irish, Italian, Jews, Protestant, and Black—with equal lack of discrimination."

Although it took some time, the gender and racial mix of the Latin School were broadened. In the difficult affirmative action years of the 1980s and 1990s, the school took it upon itself to provide minority student groups with the added assistance needed to minimize attrition rates and increase levels of academic performance.

Over the school's unparalleled history, a student's economic status was never a barrier to entry or success at the school. Today, up to a third of students qualify for free or reduced-rate meals, provided by the City of Boston. This entitlement is like, and based on, poverty measures used by government organizations.

The equality of opportunity issues, as they relate to education, have become even more important in the early years of the twenty-first century, with economists and social scientists concerned about the growing levels of inequality in our society—the widening gap between rich and poor, and the shrinking of the middle class. These experts report that economic inequality has now reached the highs of the "Great Gatsby" years during the late 1920s, and the earlier "Gilded Age" years of the 1890s. Educators are seeing the impact of these developments. Since public school funding largely comes from taxes based on home property values, it follows that more affluent communities generate higher levels of income for their students than less affluent ones. These funds are needed for the day-to-day operation of their schools, teacher salaries, extracurricular and athletic programs, special education courses, and student counseling.

The above concerns are real ones, reported in a variety of studies comparing the quality of schools in affluent suburban communities versus those of inner-city schools. No matter what communities are studied, a higher proportion of children from affluent suburban families go on to college, and to the most prestigious ones. An education at the Boston Latin School gave its students an opportunity to be an exception to this rule.

Let's take the case of a hypothetical student we will call Sasha. She is a female from a low-income minority family, and lives in the Roxbury section of Boston. She is an exceptional student, and as such, is one of twenty or more Latin School students accepted each year by Harvard College. Upon her acceptance, she submits family income data to the school, to qualify for financial aid. With her family's annual income below $65,000, at Harvard this means no payment is required at all for room, board, and tuition. The Latin School has become a gateway for Sasha, who can now start her upward climb toward realizing the American Dream.

In the context of the above, the equality of opportunity that the Latin School provides has therefore never been more important. The school does for the sons and daughters of every economic class what private schools and schools in affluent communities do for their children.

Sasha will share a Harvard dormitory room with the daughter of an affluent New York corporate attorney, and four years later march with her, in the Harvard Commencement procession. To quote Horace Mann, "Education can be the great equalizer in a society."

CONTINUITY

This attribute of the Latin School is a central reason for the school's 387-year history. It has worked to preserve the best of the past. It has established precedents and principles on which the future has been built. Continuity provides an institution with stability and reduces its vulnerability to unwarranted and haphazard change. It protects an institution against the adoption of whimsical ideas that may be in vogue one day, and out the next.

Continuity has been most evident in the Latin School curriculum. From 1635 to 1876, or for almost 250 years, the curriculum was essentially unchanged, adhering to its classical education principles. From the late 1870s, and for another 100 years, there were again few changes in the curriculum, with these being more evolutionary than revolutionary—the addition of modern languages, natural sciences, and the arts. This continuity occurred during a time when progressive education theories became widespread, and when the industrial revolution was cited as creating a need for school studies that were more practical and more occupation-oriented, than what a classical education provided.

Continuity was also the hallmark of the school during another turbulent period, when external factors outside the school's control took place. These were the years in which the Boston schools were desegregated. During this time, busing began to take place, and the Latin School and two of the other of the city's exam schools were required to adopt new affirmative action admission policies. The school made affirmative action work, but only did so by maintaining the standards and traditions of its past.

A final and important area of continuity is the role of the faculty. The term, "Memorable Masters," has been used throughout the book, with biographies of some of the most notable. While "Master" is no longer a term used in the Latin School lexicon, what each did have in common, and what continued over time, was their dedication to education that went well beyond the teaching of academic subject matter. We saw this with Ezekiel Cheever during the colonial era, and with James Lovell prior to the Revolutionary War.

What could be said for these Head Masters could also be said of the dozens of others, many with decades of tenure in the Latin School classrooms. The following eulogy to Head Master Francis Gardner, following his death in 1876 after twenty-five years at the school, could be given for any of the faculty, regardless of when they were Masters.

> Those who grew up under his care recognize that he taught them more than language, or science; since by his inspiration life took a serious and earnest purpose, and by example as well as precept he stirred them to be always thoroughly fit for any duty they undertook. Though his method was one of strict discipline and unquestioning submission to authority, it was ennobled and justified by training boys to a hearty love of sound learning, to the highest sense of honor, and a perfect loyalty to truth. No habit of deception, in word or deed, no toleration of shams, could survive his discipline and example. Patient of labor and never sparing himself, he demanded of his pupils' diligent efforts, but only to secure the full development of their own powers.

IMPORTANCE OF THE ADOLESCENT YEARS

Child psychologists define the adolescent years as generally starting between ten to twelve years of age. Latin school students entering class VI therefore spend their entire adolescence at the school. Aside from bodily changes that occur in adolescents during this period, psychologists tell us that these are the "formative" years, in terms of development of the child's cognitive and social growth. It is a period in which the child searches and tries to establish his or her identity: what to believe in, what values will become part of one's personality, and what are his or her long-term goals. In short, "Who am I, and where do I want to go?"

Adolescents, as we know, acquire virtues and values in several different ways. Parents and family are perhaps the primary source, with their influence beginning early in a child's development and continuing through maturity. For many, the church and religious training is an influence. Peers of adolescents also play an important influential role and, in the eyes of many experts, begin to compete with that of parents. Last, but not least, is the school and what is learned both in and outside the classroom.

Educators understand the importance of instilling virtues and values in students, which is termed *character education.* In the U.S., this concept dates to the colonial period with Puritan influence in schools. The widely used McGuffey Readers had moral lessons for young people. Strict school discipline also taught lessons of right and wrong, and teachers were expected to be mentors and role models, whose own virtues hopefully would be emulated by their students. Cornelia Kelley, the Latin School's first female Head of School appointed in 1986, recalled in an interview the strong belief she and her faculty had in the character education of their adolescent students. "Children came to us," she said, "with raw talent, at a very influential period in their lives; it was therefore extremely important that during this time, they be put on the right road."

The Latin School influence on a student's character starts with the fact that, in terms of the adolescent's priorities, the school is a dominant factor. The normal school year of 180 days is half the calendar year. The classroom day is then six hours, with another three hours expected to be devoted to school homework. This does not consider time spent in extracurricular activities. These classroom and non-classroom hours occur not just in a single year, but for four-to-six consecutive years, all during the formative adolescent period.

A review of the school's course materials shows the numerous situations in which character education is practiced: in literature course reading lists, and in the studies of history, languages, and other cultures. For example, students reading and discussing Dickens will find lessons of morality in his portrayal of Little Nell, Mr. Micawber, and Ebenezer Scrooge. American history courses are replete with the moral examples set by such notable figures as abolitionists Charles Sumner, Henry Ward Beecher, and Wendell Phillips.

The Latin School Classics Department describes its program and goals in the following manner:

It places young people in the ancient Greek and Roman tradition of human ideals. It uses the languages, literature, and art of those civilizations to promote, in the present one, these virtues: to restrain one's impulse to self-interest, to live and treat others with dignity, and to participate responsibly in civic life. Through careful study of excellent thought, speech, and deed from that ancient world, our students will acquire ways to understand themselves as human beings, make sense of the present, and conceive of a worthwhile future.

Beyond the morality lessons in Latin School course material, alumni today will relate story after story of classroom situations in which some of the school's Memorable Masters excelled in lessons that build character. One such story follows.

It occurred in the winter of 1949 in Room 235, where Philip Marson was Master, teaching Class II English. Each Friday, for thirty consecutive weeks, he gave his students a homework essay assignment. The essays were returned to the class by him on Monday—revised, edited, and graded, all in red ink. Obviously, he worked over every weekend to do this. Occasionally on Mondays, Marson would cite one of the better essays, and ask the student to read it out loud before the class. Today, he asked 16-year-old Sumner Ferris to do so. Sumner was a brilliant student, but he was burdened with a terrible stuttering problem and unable to get sounds out, often stammering over words and having to repeat them. But Sumner rose and began his reading. The room was silent. No one moved. All eyes were fixed on Sumner. A reading that normally would have taken five minutes, took twenty minutes. But Sumner finished and did so closing with a smile of relief and gratification.

What the Master had done was to give everyone in the classroom a lesson in character building. For Sumner, it was an exercise to build self-confidence and self-esteem. For the class, it was a demonstration of the courage, tenacity, and determination of a fellow student—one whom we would all learn to have empathy for and understanding. As a footnote, Sumner went on to Harvard, graduating with honors, and became a university English literature professor.

In other interviews with alumni, as well as retired and current faculty, three virtues are cited most often as unique to the Latin School experience—one that left an indelible and lifelong influence on its graduates. These include restraining one's impulse to self-interest, living and treating others with dignity, and participating responsibly in civic life.

THE LOVE OF LEARNING

In September of 1929, an eleven-year-old son of Russian Jewish immigrants entered the Latin School. He, like other Latin School pupils at the time, would use his school education as a stepping-stone to a life far better than those of his immigrant parents. The student's name was Leonard Bernstein, who later became one of the twentieth century's most renowned musical composers and conductors, with works encompassing symphonic music, stage musicals, ballet, and film.

While at the Latin School, Bernstein couldn't study music, as it was not yet in the curriculum, even though he had been learning to play the piano a year before entering the school. But a musical education could wait. The Latin School would now provide a foundation of learning for him, one that could be applied to any field of endeavor. Twenty-five years after graduating from the Latin School, Bernstein wrote a foreword to a book written by one of the memorable Latin School Masters under whom he had studied. This Master was Philip Marson, and the foreword spoke to the value of education beyond the mundane: "He taught me something unique, incomparable, and invaluable in education, far beyond the teaching of tetrameter or dangling particles, or even the glories of English verse; he taught me how to learn."

In alumni interviews, life-long learning is one of the most frequently mentioned lessons that the Latin School bestowed upon its students. Alumni say it is a virtue that has its own intrinsic rewards—the passion, joy, and satisfaction of learning, for learning's sake. In another sense, it is a virtue that has practical and personal relevance. Today we live in a knowledge-based economy, one in which lifelong learning is essential. Globalization and new technologies require business executives to learn new ways of doing business. In medicine, breakthroughs in biotechnology require doctors to learn new patient treatment procedures. For those in the legal profession, new precedents set by the courts require study and interpretation. In these and other occupations, learning cannot end when one's formal education ends. It must become a lifelong habit, and the earlier this habit is learned, the better.

The Latin School has been able to instill this virtue in its students in several different ways—both in the classroom, and out of the classroom. This virtue was one that was modelled by the Memorable Masters themselves. Most were scholars who demonstrated their love for learning by walking the walk. Students throughout most of the twentieth century all remember Max Levine, for example, who earned the designation "Mr. Latin School," for his more than 60-year involvement with the school as student, Master, and eventually active alumnus.

Mr. Levine, a Jewish immigrant from Poland, arrived in the country just prior to the turn of the century, and was enrolled in the Latin School in 1901. After six years at the school, he went on to Harvard, graduating with honors in Latin and Greek. In 1915, he joined the Latin School faculty, and for the next forty-five years taught Classics, and then French, as a department head. His former students remember how in the classroom, his eyes peered through rimless glasses, and how his facial expressions reflected the joy of what he was doing, along with his love of scholarship, his love of learning, and his reverence for men of learning. Max Levine turned what could have been tedious days of learning a foreign language into a daily delight. His class opened with his classic greeting *Bon jour, monsieurs,* and closed with *Au revoir, monsieurs."* He took you to France and home again every day, and you, as he did, loved the journey.

Outside the classroom, there have been other ways that the Latin School built love of learning into its pupils. Many of these have existed for years; others are relatively new. Clubs are the oldest, and a gathering place where, after the class day has ended, like-minded students can pursue a variety of different academic and non-academic learning interests, for example, an astrology club, a Bible club, a computer society, or an economics club. In September of each year, a Club Fair is held where each of up to 100 clubs make presentations to prospective members.

The school library is another resource that both symbolizes and encourages the love of learning. The Keefe Memorial Library is a unique facility, opened in 2000. It was largely financed through a $3 million gift from Harry V. Keefe, Jr., Latin School Class of 1939. Mr. Keefe was a highly successful Wall Street banker and generous philanthropist. The library is a 12,500 square foot facility with an impressive two-story vaulted reading room, wood bookcases, and high-quality library tables with individual reading lights. It has the look and feel of an Ivy League college library.

Every educator knows that students learn and enjoy learning by undertaking their own research projects. The Latin School requires that each junior and senior complete a research paper, much like that of a college thesis. Science classes all encourage student participation in outside student fairs, as well as its own annual Science Fair.

The encouragement of reading habits is another goal of the school, as a lifelong reader is a lifelong learner. Outside reading is a requirement in almost every course. Additionally, fiction and nonfiction summer reading is mandatory for every student. Reading lists are provided, and students are accountable for having read one or more of the prescribed books, prior to return to school in September.

Whether it be the way course material is taught, the important role of the Latin School Masters, or through the availability of after-class learning resources, alumni all take pride in having learned how to learn at the Latin School.

WORK ETHIC

Any discussion with a Latin School alumni will uncover the presence of a remarkable work ethic. Alumni will quickly point out that they learned this work ethic to be more than a means to an end, but rather as a moral virtue that enables them to take deep pride in "a job well done" and to nurture and expect this quality in others as well.

Work ethic, as with other virtues, has multiple dimensions. It is built on diligence, ambition, industriousness, determination, perseverance, and commitment. It requires one to be resourceful, conscientious, and possess tenacity. Those with a strong work ethic are reliable and dependable. They can be counted on to do a job and do it well. And the existence of a strong work ethic is one of the cornerstones of the American Dream. Alexis de Tocqueville recognized its prevalence in the U.S. as early as the nineteenth century. Social scientists cite it as a unique American virtue and one that has contributed to our nation's preeminence among other nations of the world.

Unlike most other virtues that have been discussed, it may come as some surprise that work ethic does not have ancient Greek or Roman roots. In both these societies, work was for slaves to perform, and was in fact looked down upon. Freemen engaged in other pursuits in the fields of commerce, the arts, or just leisure itself.

Although the Romans built a massive and sprawling empire with roads, bridges, and public buildings, all the work was done by slaves. Low regard for work continued in European societies into the medieval period. Peasants were the tenant farm workers, and for them, work just meant subsistence, and not upward mobility in their aristocratic and feudal societies.

It was not until the sixteenth century, and the Protestant Reformation, where work began to be seen as a virtue. Some of this shift was driven by Martin Luther, the German theologian, who challenged the Catholic belief that gratification exists only in the hereafter. He saw the role of man as one of serving God, and doing the work of God, here on Earth. Work was seen as one's "calling," giving it an infusion of spiritual dignity. Following Luther,

John Calvin, a French theologian, spoke of work as "the will of God," promoting that "work was virtuous." The teachings of Calvin, later known as Calvinism, became the basic tenet on which Protestant virtues and values subsequently were built in New England. The Latin School's Ben Franklin, who helped shape the American Dream, included several work ethic aphorisms in his famous list of thirteen virtues. One of these was *Resolution,* where he encouraged us to, "resolve to perform what you ought; and perform without fail what you resolve."

The most noted analysis of the historical roots of the work ethic was done in 1904 by Max Weber, a German economist and social scientist. With the publication of his book *The Protestant Ethic and the Spirit of Capitalism,* he tied together the religious work ethic tenets of Calvinism and Puritanism with the economic success of capitalism. It is interesting to note that in Weber's well-researched book, he cites the serious contribution that Benjamin Franklin made in helping establish the virtues of a work ethic. Too often, we think of Franklin's sayings as just simple and homespun aphorisms, where they should be considered quite insightful and scholarly.

It was Franklin who took what many perceived as virtues based on religious beliefs, and turned them into every day, practical lessons of morality, ones that everyone could understand. Franklin died in 1790, at the age of 84. His famous autobiography that contained his morality lessons was published in France a year later. The first English edition appeared in 1793. Popular throughout the nineteenth century, it was no doubt read by thousands of Latin School students in the years that followed its publication. These students may have gotten some of their work ethic lessons from his writings, but their work ethic lessons also came in many other important ways.

The sizable academic workload of the Latin School itself demanded hard work. The curriculum today calls for five courses each year in Classes VI and V and six courses in Classes IV to I, rather than the four normally required in most secondary schools. And the six hours of daily class time are supplemented by three hours of nightly homework, for which students are accountable the next morning.

Typical of the workload in a single year's course during the 1950s is that which the Master in English, Philip Marson, humbly described to his students.

I pointed out at the beginning of the term what my classes could expect: weekly themes, study of prescribed books; collateral reading of three novels, three plays, one volume of verse by a poet of each pupil's own choice, and one biography; and a full written report for each work read. While outlining this course, I made clear to my students that I was not piling on unnecessary burdens just to keep them busy. After all, they would have only about thirty themes, about eighteen reports on books, and ten trial questions on the works studied in class. Nobody whimpered, wailed, or gnashed his teeth.

To achieve a passing grade in courses such as Marson's, hard work would be the only answer. Sheer intelligence would not be enough. As Thomas Edison once said, "Genius is one percent inspiration, and ninety-nine percent perspiration." Deadlines have always been part of the Latin School's educational practices: daily, weekly, monthly, and end-of-term—each usually with a test and a grade. You were accountable to yourself, to the Master, and your parents. That's what a strong work ethic demanded.

Disciplinary practices also help establish a work ethic. Tardiness was punished by after-school detention. When the class bell rings, you had better be in your seat, ready to go. No excuses. Alumni today joke with one another about how they learned punctuality lessons, one of the values implicit in a work ethic. They say that if you make a business or social appointment with a fellow alumnus, you can always be sure they will be on time.

There were therefore a variety of ways that one learned about and acquired a strong work ethic. Each lesson is added to another, and when the lessons are practiced daily, they become habit, become internalized, and ingrained in one's character. What became instilled in one's formative adolescent years, subsequently became lifelong virtues and values.

SELF-DISCIPLINE

Perhaps one of the most important virtues that the Latin School instilled in its graduates is *self-discipline.* In a broader sense, a set of positive, self-imposed behavioral disciplines, which an individual applies to everyday life. Self-discipline requires an understanding of right and wrong, and carries with it, accountability to oneself. Latin School's notable nineteenth-century alumnus, Henry Ward Beecher, summed up what he believed self-discipline required: "Hold yourself responsible for a higher standard than anybody else expects of you; never excuse yourself, never pity yourself; be a hard master to yourself, and be lenient to everyone else."

What must not be overlooked, however, is the role that the school's disciplinary practices played in creating habits of self-discipline. Clearly, rules and regulations can serve as valuable teaching lessons when it comes to practicing self-discipline. As is customary with most every higher education institution, at the start of each school year, each Latin School student is provided with a forty-page student handbook. It includes the school's disciplinary rules, procedures, and types of punishment for infractions. It also includes an honor code calling for a pledge to "uphold the Boston Latin School values of honor and integrity."

Misdemeanor marks, like demerits used in the military academies, have been the long-standing means imposed for minor infractions. Their use at the school dates to the early nineteenth century. Today's handbook still lists sixteen of those infractions as examples of violations of the school's code of conduct. They include speaking out of turn, improper dress, and boisterousness in the classroom. Issued by faculty, the accumulation of five or more misdemeanor marks during a marking term will result in a failing grade in conduct.

Detention, before or after school, is another enforcement tool used by faculty. Students are expected to be punctual and in their homeroom seats by 7:45 a.m. If not, they must report for detention on the next school day at 7:00 a.m. Punctuality is clearly a virtue expected of every student, and Latin School students learn this early in life.

Rules related to classroom behavior, the dining hall, use of the library, gymnasium, and other facilities have one implicit lesson in common—teaching students respect for one another, respect for faculty, and respect for their learning environment. Adherence to the school's rules and regulations is expected of every student, with the goal that appropriate behavior become ingrained in students. In the words of Aristotle, "We are what we repeatedly do; excellence then is not an act, but a habit."

Major infractions are listed in the school handbook; they include lying, cheating, using offensive language, disruption of classes, bullying, or harassment, to name just a few. These infractions are punishable by censure, suspension, and even expulsion. Censure is the official school reprimand that is sent to the parents and must be returned signed. In the administration of the school's code of conduct, faculty always make it clear that the code is not an arbitrary set of rules demanding obedience, but rather a set of standards and expectations built on positive virtues that every student should possess as he or she moves into adulthood.

Self-discipline, along with a strong work ethic and a love of learning, were the top three virtues Latin School alumni cited most often as their most memorable lessons—not taught as subject matter, but rather by the example set by the school's faculty. Curriculum and classroom went beyond academic material. It taught right from wrong. From its inception, the school believed strongly in character education—well before modern-day educators adopted this as curriculum.

It was noted earlier that each year during Commencement Week, the Latin School awards more than sixty prizes and medals to students drawn from all the six classes. One would expect that these awards would recognize academic excellence. Not so. There are just as many awards for qualities of character as there are for academic excellence. Funded largely by alumni benefactors, the prizes and medals reflect what these alumni believe is important to the school, its students, and their own legacy.

While in times past, the Latin School Student Handbook was largely focused on rules designed to enforce discipline, it has since evolved into a kinder, gentler platform—providing students with principles and core values to help them assimilate and become more essential and productive members of their school community and beyond. These core values, reflected in the acronym T.H.R.I.V.E., include general guiding principles such as:

- **Together** we are stronger.
- **Honor** our history, speak truth to the present and lead into the future.
- **Respect** each other, respect our unique identities, and respect the fundamental humanity of each person.
- **Impact** the world, locally and globally.
- **Value** our bodies, minds, and holistic well-being.
- **Embody** excellence through our efforts and deeds.

CHAPTER IX:

Individual Needs and Special Interests

If a man does not keep pace with his companions, perhaps it is because he hears a different drummer. Let him step to the music he hears, however measured or far away.

—HENRY DAVID THOREAU

DEEPLY ROOTED IN THE AMERICAN culture is the importance of individual self-expression—the ability to pursue one's own interests and the right to develop and express one's own views. Our Declaration of Independence speaks of the "unalienable rights" of the individual. Historian Frederick Jackson Turner maintained that it was the rugged individualism and self-initiative which we saw on the American frontier that did so much to build our nation.

Some of the best writings on the importance of the individual in a democratic society were done by philosopher and Latin School alumnus Ralph Waldo Emerson. Historian Samuel Eliot Morison said of Emerson, "If Jefferson was the prophet of democracy, and Jackson its hero, Emerson was its high priest." One of Emerson's most famous essays was entitled *Self-Reliance.* In it, the author spoke of the innate ability and unlimited potential of individuals themselves, and the importance of self-fulfillment. He saw free-thinking and non-conformity as essential to human growth. He repeatedly used his now well-known phrase, "Trust thyself."

An issue to grapple with is the degree to which the historical classical education of the Latin School has addressed the needs of the individual, and how the school is responding to these needs today. Much of the criticism of the school has centered around its shortfall in recognizing the needs of the individual as it relates to self-expression and nonconformity.

CLASSICAL EDUCATION VS INDIVIDUALITY

There is no question that, despite modest changes made in the Latin School curriculum over time, to this day, it could be characterized as rigid and uniform, with most every academic course being mandatory. Even in situations where there were electives, the choices open to students were narrow ones. This top-down standardization lasted well into the latter years of the twentieth century.

There have always been strong arguments for curriculum uniformity and consistency.

First, it was a college preparatory curriculum that required a firm grounding in academic fundamentals necessary for college entrance. Many of these requirements were set by the colleges themselves—particularly Harvard, where so many Latin School graduates were accepted for admissions. For students in Boston not planning to attend college, there were other public-school options open to them, where course offerings were much broader.

The strongest historical argument in support of the Latin School classical curriculum was that it did, in fact, succeed without inhibiting opportunities for individual expression, pursuit of special interests, and creativity. The proof of this can be witnessed by what many of the school's most prominent pupils were able to accomplish in their lifetime, in a variety of different fields of endeavor, where unique and individual talents were necessary.

Charles Bulfinch, an eighteenth-century Latin School alumnus, became the country's most prominent American-born architect. Even though he never took a course in design or drawing at the Latin School, what he took from his classical education was the strength and eminence of ancient Greek and Roman cultures. He is largely credited with introducing neoclassical architecture in our country, all based on Greek and Roman architectural concepts. This unique style during this period is reflected in his work on Faneuil Hall, the Massachusetts State House, as well as the Capitol building in Washington, DC.

George Santayana, a noted philosopher, essayist, poet, and nineteenth-century Latin School alumnus, found his avenue for self-expression as the founding editor of the school's magazine, *The Latin School Register*. The publication began in 1882 and is still in existence today. Arthur Fiedler, an early twentieth-century alumnus, only began the study of music after he left the Latin School. Later he enjoyed a fifty-year career as conductor of the Boston Pops Orchestra. Yes, he was a musician, but he had a broader range of interests and talents in understanding American cultural tastes. On July 4, 1976, he led the nation's bicentennial celebration in Boston, with a gathering of 400,000 celebrants on the city's Charles River Esplanade. Appropriately, the concert closed with his signature orchestral rendering of *Stars and Stripes Forever*. The following year, he was presented the Presidential Medal of Freedom by President Gerald Ford.

For these self-expressionists, and other less prominent Latin School alumni, the school provided an important foundation on which one's own individuality could later be expressed. As Leonard Bernstein told us in the previous chapter, as students they were taught to learn, with the lessons applicable to any and every area of individual interest or endeavor.

THE LATIN SCHOOL TODAY

If Latin School alumnus Charles William Eliot were alive today, he would be proud to see that the core curriculum he promoted—one built on a firm foundation of language, history, mathematics, and science studies—was still intact. At the turn of the twentieth century, Eliot was one of the nation's leading educators, heading the National Education Association (NEA) and its *Committee of Ten*. The group carefully studied and recommended uniform standards of secondary education throughout the country. His curriculum recommendations were quite different from those of a later NEA study group. That group's study report, *Cardinal Principles of Secondary Education,* advocated a curriculum whose prime focus would be almost exclusively on individual needs and special interests—a la carte-style curriculum, dominated by electives, and a wide range of non-academic, occupation-oriented subjects. The Eliot point of view, expressed in *The Committee of Ten Report*, clearly stated that in a high school curriculum, "Occupational decisions should be put off until after graduation."

The Latin School of today recognizes, now more than ever, the importance of catering to the individual needs and interests of its students, balancing its curriculum, without diluting or compromising its historic foundation. There are now far more elective options open to students than there ever have been before. However, what these electives set out to do is deepen and enrich students' knowledge in each subject area. This is done by offering second, third, and even fourth-level courses, beyond basic courses. Another characteristic that sets the Latin School's electives apart from those of other schools is that they are all academic courses. Non-academic electives which are so prevalent in many schools that are less rigorous are not available to students at the Latin School.

The Latin School also recognizes that there may be differences in levels of academic achievement among students. Twenty-four Advanced Placement program electives are therefore available to students. The school offers courses in more than two-thirds of the subjects in the College Board's Advanced Placement program. What's more, the Latin School provides student instructions selecting courses that best reflect what students know about themselves. Some of the guidance provided includes:

- Consider any academic or career interests you may have.

- Think about areas where you feel as though you could challenge yourself.

- Consider your time management skills and how you will be able to handle more hours dedicated to homework.

GUIDANCE AND TUTORING

Up until the late twentieth century, the Latin School largely practiced a "sink or swim" philosophy with its students. A surprisingly high percentage of entering students failed to graduate from the school and had to transfer to less demanding neighborhood high schools. There was no tutoring available at the time. Guidance counseling was limited to advice relating to one's post-high school years, rather than the challenges and difficulties that students faced while attending the Latin School. This "sink or swim" practice no longer exists today, replaced more by a "we'll teach you to swim" philosophy. The school's retention rate is now around 85 percent. Retention has clearly replaced rejection.

Restructured during the Cornelia Kelley administration, the Guidance Department now has a full-time team of nine counselors, headed by a Program Director. Entering Class VI students are assigned to a guidance counselor with whom they will work during their first two years at the school. These boys and girls, usually aged eleven and twelve, are in their formative adolescent years, just beginning to find themselves in a new school environment, and the counselors recognize the transition support needs of these students. The elementary school that they have left behind is usually a smaller one than the 2,400-student Latin School. It is probably not as ethnically and racially diverse as the Latin School, which draws its pupils from all parts of the city, rather than a small and perhaps homogeneous neighborhood. And, these new Latin School students find that, for the first time, they are now competing academically with the best and brightest of pupils from all parts of the city. At their elementary school, they may have been at the top tier academically; now every one of their fellow students is top tier.

After moving on to the high school level, students are still assigned to a counselor, but this may be on a rotating basis. Though transition support needs may now be behind them, the counselor still provides important support in other areas—helping students understand their capabilities and limitations, improving their study habits, dealing with the problems of failing or at-risk students. For upper-class students, counsel is provided on college selection and financial aid availability. The counselors plan and coordinate school visits by college admission personnel. All these counseling activities work to keep the school's retention rate at a high level. They act as a safety net, in what is a very demanding school environment.

Within the school's Guidance Department, there is a separate and distinct entity called the McCarthy Institute for Transition and Support. Its primary responsibility is conducting the school's tutoring programs. It is almost totally financed by the alumni's Boston Latin School Association (BLSA). The salary of its faculty-member head, and program expenses, are supported by the BLSA. Currently, the BLSA provides approximately $2.5M in program support. The school's public funds only provide the space for the program.

After-school tutoring is one of its two major tutoring efforts. It is available on a walk-in basis four days weekly. Two classrooms are used, one for general subjects, the other for math, science, and Latin on a rotating weekday basis. Though there is a lead faculty tutor, all other tutors are volunteer upper-class students.

The second program is the Saturday Success School, conducted on twenty Saturday mornings beginning in October. Participating students select three courses in which they want to improve their performance, and forty-five minutes of tutoring then are scheduled for each. Tutoring is on a one-on-one basis, with alumni tutors or students from the local area colleges. All work on a non-paid volunteer basis.

The school's tutoring programs are not just for students having difficulty with their academic subjects. Many attends with a goal of improving their proficiency and their grade performance. The Institute also provides other special programs. For Class II junior-year students, it has a nine-week program to help them in choosing colleges and prepare their applications for entry and scholarships. As the Institute indicates in its name, it addresses the dual needs of students both in transition and support.

VISUAL AND PERFORMING ARTS

There is no area of study in which individuality is most evident than in the visual and performing arts. It is here that originality, creativity, and self-expression come alive—in one's paintings, sculpture, or on-stage in a theatrical performance. It is an area of study characterized by self-discovery and self-fulfillment.

There is also evidence today that participation in the arts by adolescents works to improve their performance in other academic areas. In 2002, the Arts Education Partnership (AEP), a non-profit group of organizations interested in art education, reported findings from more than sixty research studies. The report showed that, "Arts participation and education are associated with improved cognitive, social, and behavioral outcomes in individuals." The cognitive skills cited were perception, reasoning, judgment, and memory; the social and behavioral skills were empathy, collaboration, and understanding of others. The findings reflect the multi-faceted benefits of art education—its positive influence on academic skills, and in the building of character.

In an earlier chapter that dealt with Latin School's academic program was a discussion of the course offerings on the Visual and Performing Arts Department. It noted that there are fourteen courses offered in four art areas—visual arts, instrumental music, vocal music, and drama. The department is headed by a Program Director with nine faculty members.

The music programs encompass a wide array of formats, and varied choices within each format. For example, in the instrumental music category, there are three areas of orchestral study—concert strings, philharmonic strings, and repertory. There are three band choices. Vocal music has programs in concert and repertory choices, as well as chamber, show, and gospel choir.

Visual arts and drama classes are given in Classes VI and V, and while there are no formal courses later, students have opportunities for guided self-study or group instructional sessions, held on a regular basis. Advanced Placement Visual Art and Advanced Placement Music are available in Classes II and I, and drama opportunities for all are available after school hours. The Boston Latin Theatre Company also has stage performances each year and has a fully equipped stage rehearsal facility.

Though art programs are one of the first areas where cost-conscious administrators usually make budget cuts, the Latin School has been able to continue, and even enlarge its program, through alumni funding and the work of the BLSA. The school's art program compares favorably with those of the best suburban schools that have the benefit of higher levels of public funding.

EXTRACURRICULAR PROGRAMS

In interviews conducted for the preparation of this book, one of the faculty members commented that, "It seems that on many days there are as many pupils here in the school after the class day has ended as during the class day itself." These after-hours pupils are the participants in the school's numerous and diverse extracurricular activities. Many of these students can be seen on the Visual and Performing Arts floors, others in club meetings, and at athletic team practices. What these programs all have in common is that they are avenues for self-expression and pursuit of one's own special interests.

The Latin School Student Handbook lists more than seventy-five clubs open to students and include clubs whose student special interests might lie in the arts, sports, health and fitness, or ethnicity—to name just a few of the major categories of clubs.

The school's interscholastic sports program is also an extensive one. It was once limited to just five sports: football, baseball, basketball, hockey, and track. There are now fourteen team sports, with the addition of such sports as wrestling, swimming, soccer, volleyball, sailing, crew, tennis, fencing, lacrosse, and golf. Grouped as Fall, Winter, and Spring sports, there are both varsity and junior varsity teams in most of the sports. Exclusive girls' teams are listed for eight sports. Though most public middle schools do not have, or cannot afford, sports program for these students, the Latin School does have them—funded by its alumni association.

Eligibility for participation in a sports team requires passing grades in five major subjects for Classes IV-Class I and in four major subjects for Class VI and Class V. The same eligibility policy covers participating in all extracurricular activities and competitions including clubs, academic teams, dramatics, and music. In effect, the school is saying "Yes, pursuit of your own special interests in our school's programs is important, but not at the expense of compromising our academic standards."

In following its philosophy of a contemporary classical education, this chapter has shown how the school now blends the strengths of a classical education with its emphasis on fundamentals, with the needs students may have in the pursuit of their own special interests. The latter is done through more electives in the curriculum, tutoring, and guidance for students in need of special assistance, and Advanced Placement courses for others who excel in their studies. Other opportunities for self-expression and individuality are now available through the new Visual and Performing Arts program and expanded after-school activities in special interest clubs and athletics. Whatever the deficiencies may have been in a pure classical education, today the Latin School has more than made up for them with its contemporary classical curriculum that addresses the needs of the whole individual.

CHAPTER X:

Preserving the School Legacy and the Dream

Your descendants shall gather your fruits.

—VIRGIL

IN 1844, A FEW YEARS after the Latin School celebrated its 200th birthday, a small group of alumni and former faculty founded what is known today as the Boston Latin School Association (BLSA). As an active alumnus and one of the Association's officers, Charles William Eliot described its purpose: "To maintain the school's prestige, to keep its glories untarnished, to augment its efficiency, and add to its renown." One of its earliest undertakings was the funding of a school library that would contain school memorabilia and collections of important classical works.

The new association was a volunteer organization, and remained so until the mid-1980s, when a full-time staff was first hired. The current mission statement outlines four goals for the organization:

1. Preserve and support the mission and excellence of the Boston
    Latin School.

2. Build and maintain relationships among the school's alumni and friends.

3. Raise funds for both the school and Association activities.

4. Serve as an effective model of a successful public school—private association partnership.

The Association, headquartered in downtown Boston, is headed by a president, Peter G. Kelly, who was appointed in June of 2009. A 1983 Latin School graduate, he had previously been an Assistant Dean for development and alumni relations at Boston University.

The Association has a volunteer Board of Trustees and twelve standing committees overseeing such activities as communications, development, finance, and endowment investments. It draws on the varied professional expertise of its alumni for these committee positions.

Membership in the association is comprised of alumni, former faculty members, and families and friends of the school. It totals more than 16,000, with computer databases containing contact information on each member. Also included, upon voluntary submission by individual members, are the member's education information, occupation, and business profiles. Though fundraising for the support of the school and its students is the Association's most important function, it engages in a whole host of other activities. These include planning of alumni reunions, coordination of regional chapter activities, awards dinners, alumni news publications, and a BLSA/BLS website.

FUNDRAISING

The public school system in the U.S. was founded on the principle that it would be fully funded by the public, and the U.S. Constitution places this responsibility on the states. Though the federal government provides special grants to the states and local communities, state and local taxes are the primary source of funding.

Since the founding of the BLSA in 1844, it has been the belief of its membership that private funds could supplement public funding and work to (a) enhance the quality of an education provided to Latin School students, and (b) provide scholarship monies for talented graduates going on to colleges and universities. This is an unusual undertaking for a public school, one largely limited to private secondary schools, colleges, and universities.

For most of the Latin School's early history, there were no organized fundraising efforts. There were individual bequests from alumni, or scholarship endowments set up in the name of the benefactor. For example, alumnus Joseph P. Kennedy, on the fiftieth anniversary of his graduation, in 1958 established a $50,000 scholarship fund in his name.

It was not until 1978 that the then BLSA president, Stanley Miller, BLS 1948, formalized fundraising, introducing an Annual Fund Drive. A few years earlier, the BLS Foundation was formed, with its sole focus on funding issues. Still limited in scope, both efforts were largely individual undertakings, usually with one-on-one solicitation of potential benefactors on behalf of the school. It was not until the BLSA became fully staffed that more organized efforts began. It was also strengthened and unified by the 1997 merger of the BLS Foundation and the BLSA. The next years would then see more aggressive efforts, including Pons Privatus, which concluded in 2004, and was defined as a private bridge for public good—the first-ever capital campaign established on behalf of a public school. *Pon Privatus* was followed by a much larger campaign in 2012, known as the *Prima Perpetua* Campaign, which raised over $54M—the largest fundraising effort ever undertaken by a public high school.

PUBLIC FUNDING LIMITATIONS

Data from the U.S. Department of Education show that funding for public education comes from three major sources. Though it varies by year, states and local communities generally provide 95 percent; the federal government 5 percent. State funds are generated from personal income taxes, corporate taxes, sales taxes, fees, and local revenues, largely from property taxes.

The early years of the twenty-first century have seen downward pressures on two of the three public education funding sources—state and local funds. Weak economic growth and resulting declines in tax collections have forced states to cap or reduce the funding that they provide to their local school districts. At the same time, declining real estate values and homeowner resistance to higher property taxes have cut into the local funds available for public schools.

In this climate of state and local budget austerity, modest increases in federal funding support have occurred, but they are insignificant in terms of most local school district needs. Though some might argue that these budget constraints are a function of short-term economic factors, others believe that limitations in public funding for education will continue. Though school enrollments will continue to rise, economic constraints will limit the availability of public funds available for schools.

In Boston, budgets for individual schools are set each fiscal year. Funds allocated to the school are for teacher salaries, administration, and supplies. Separate city budgets are established for maintenance of the buildings, utilities, and other facility-related expenses. A school's budget is developed using a "per pupil" formula that considers the number of pupils and their basic educational needs. It is then adjusted, or "weighted," by factors that address special educational needs and higher expenses normally associated with them (i.e., the presence of disadvantaged or handicapped students, English language learners, and vocational students). Though every school would like to see more public funding, unfortunately our nation's priorities set limits on the funds available for education. In 2022, Boston's major league baseball team, the Red Sox, paid one player Chris Sale—their starting pitcher—a salary more than three times what the entire 132-person Latin School faculty is paid.

The combined external factors that are now at work suggest a growing need for the Latin School to generate higher levels of private funding. It is here that the alumni, represented by the BLSA, must be called upon if the Latin School legacy and the American Dream are to be kept alive. These funding needs are not for frivolous or for so-called niceties; they are for the essentials that make the Latin School education what it is. Let's look at the varied list of needs that this funding provides.

BLSA SUPPORT ACTIVITIES

There are three categories of funding that the alumni and the BLSA use to support the Latin School: (1) supplements to its programs budget, (2) scholarship funding, (3) capital projects funding.

Program Budget Supplements

In Fiscal Year 2019-2020, over $1.4 million was provided to the school by the BLSA. The supplements serve to enhance the Latin School experience for its students, taking it beyond what would normally exist in other of the city's high schools. Funds are used to enhance the learning environment and experience. A walk through the third-floor science wing of the school will reveal laboratories with BLSA-funded lab equipment, microscopes, laser equipment, and other sophisticated test devices. Again, these are largely BLSA-funded. The first-floor Keefe Memorial Library, named for its benefactor, receives an annual stipend for library and media technology updates. Next to the library is the office of the school's archivist, whose salary is fully paid by the BLSA.

In a visit to the Visual and Performing Arts wing of the school, one will see shelves with stacks of supplies for after-school use in ceramics, painting, and photography—all largely financed from BLSA funds. Productions of theatrical performances require licensing fees, and these are absorbed by the BLSA, as are entry fees for musical competitions, and student transportation to the events. For those interested in writing and journalism, the school's student publications provide this opportunity—again, largely through BLSA funding.

The school would not be able on its own to have the fifteen-sport athletic program that it does without alumni support. This includes funding for freshman and junior varsity sports, coaching, sports equipment, and team bus transportation. Funding for upgrades to its athletics facilities, including the weight room and training areas, are underway.

The guidance and tutoring programs—an integral part of the school's philosophy—give every student the opportunity to succeed and receives extensive funding from the BLSA. The salary of the McCarthy Institute director is fully paid by the BLSA, as well as expenses for both the after-school tutoring and the Saturday Success School programs. Endowments will also be used to secure robust student mental health service.

Finally, to advance the educational development of students, there are summer fellowship stipends. For the faculty, there are funds set aside for professional development, which ultimately accrue to the benefit of students.

There is a Director of Technology whose salary is paid from an endowment bequest by Andrew J. Viterbi, BLS Class of 1952; this position looks to the future needs of the school. He was one of the founders of Qualcomm, a Fortune 500 company that pioneered cellular communication. He received the school's Distinguished Graduate of the Year Award in 2006. In his acceptance remarks, he warmly thanked the Latin School for how much it did for him. Born to a Jewish family in Italy, he escaped Europe just days before World War II began. Viterbi spoke of the school's important role "in opening the doors of American opportunity to the children of immigrants, like me." A few years later, the endowment he established for the school was his way of saying, "thank you."

During time spent at the school in research for this book, and in interviews conducted with the school's department heads, it became clear that without the BLSA alumni support, the Latin School would not be what it has been, and now is. It would be just an ordinary school, not the extraordinary one that it continues to be. This private support funding works to make the Latin School competitive with the best suburban and private college preparatory schools.

Scholarship Funding

Virtually all those graduating from the Latin School go on to college. These graduates all have the intelligence and the talent that enable them to succeed in college. Many have already demonstrated this through the Advanced Placement programs. Average SAT scores also are well above the national averages. There are therefore no academic barriers to their college acceptance. What the school's guidance counselors have said is that it is cost that is the real barrier, and a key determinant in the student's choice of colleges. It is easy to understand why. The College Board reports that in 2021, tuition, fees, books, and room and board at four-year state universities, averages more than $27,000 a year for in-state students, and over $44,000 for out-of-state; and at private universities, over $50,000 all in. The median household income for families in the city of Boston is just $71,000. This is less than half of what more prosperous suburban Boston households earn. Financial aid is therefore a necessity for virtually all but the sons and daughters of affluent families.

Fortunately, the Latin School alumni recognize this need and have been generous in their support. Under the management of the BLSA, $750,000 is provided in scholarship support, funded by endowments. In 2020, income from endowment reached over $3M. Endowment income is often used for scholarships for graduating seniors. The scholarships are awarded for financial need; academic achievement and promise; character traits such as leadership and commitment; achievement in areas of special interest—e.g., athletics, music, and the arts; and there are scholarships that say something about the school and its legacy:

> *This scholarship is awarded for a college-bound scholar whose parents or grandparents were immigrants, and who appreciate a Latin School education as an end in itself, as well as a means to an end.*

—The Yee Family Scholarship

Capital Funds

By the late 1980s, the Latin School's Avenue Louis Pasteur facility was badly in need of repair. It had been 40 years since its last renovation. This need gave birth in 2000 to the *Pons Privatus* capital campaign, noted earlier in this chapter. It was the first ever capital fundraising program undertaken by a public school. Though the City of Boston is responsible for its school structures and sets aside funds for renovation and repair, these were supplemented by alumni gifts, obtained as part of the school's capital fundraising efforts.

The Keefe Memorial Library was one of the additions largely funded by an alumnus whom we met earlier. Without his funding, the city certainly would have reconstructed or built a new library, but it would have been an ordinary one, not the extraordinary facility that now exists.

Looking to the future, the school will face new and changing facility needs, and while public funds may be earmarked for some of these needs, it is unlikely that they will all be met by public funding—particularly for a school that sets its standards as high as the Latin School does.

PRESERVING THE LEGACY

Though there are numerous ways the legacy of the Latin School can be preserved, financial support is one of the most important ways to accomplish this objective. On the positive side, the school is fortunate to have an alumni body that stands ready to provide its support.

Preservation of this legacy for future generations is important to these alumni. It's what enabled them to realize the American Dream, and they see it as their obligation to ensure that it is there for future generations. Michael Leven, Class of 1955, and a generous donor, says he sees himself as a debtor, with his gifts to repay the school. "Without the Latin School," he says, "I have serious doubts that I would be sitting in this chair." The chair he was referring to was one as CEO of a billion-dollar multinational company. Leven says, "Writing a donation check to the Latin School is like writing a thank-you note."

This book opened with a simple proclamation-like statement of what is meant by the American Dream. Our book now closes with a statement on the role Boston Latin School has played for me in fulfilling that dream for so many of its graduates. In this statement, I believe that I am expressing the deep-rooted feelings of many of my fellow alumni.

Boston Latin
School Manifesto

WE THE ALUMNI OF THE Boston Latin School want to express our gratitude for the rewarding educational experience that the school provided us during our formative adolescent years.

We are grateful, in the true spirit of the American Dream, that the doors of opportunity were open to all of us—regardless of race, religion, ethnicity, or economic background.

We learned that the lessons of the Latin School went far beyond what was written in our textbooks. We acquired important lifelong skills in critical thinking—learning how to reason, analyze, synthesize, and prioritize. We found opportunities to express our individuality and creativity in the school's many and varied extracurricular programs.

We are deeply indebted to what we term, our Memorable Masters, who were not only teachers, but mentors and role models as well. They were all masters of their subject matter, but also individuals who worked every day to build long-lasting values in all of us—a love of learning, a strong work ethic, personal integrity, and self-discipline.

We take pride in the traditions of the school—its long and proud history, with its many eminent graduates who symbolized and shaped the American Dream. We have admiration for the school's ability to maintain an unwavering allegiance to its deep-rooted core values in the face of changes that occurred over time in our nation's educational philosophy and institutions of learning. When change and transition were necessary, it was never disruptive and, in the end, strengthened the school's commitment to its students.

We are thankful for all these many gifts that have enabled us to realize the American Dream, to lead fuller and richer lives. And because of what the Latin School has done for us, we resolve to preserve its legacy for others, who may follow in our footsteps in pursuit of their own dreams.

Education is the gateway to the American Dream. The Puritan settlers knew this, and so did our Founding Fathers. They saw education as a means to an end, providing individuals with the knowledge and skills needed to realize their full potential and to contribute to the sustainability of our nation. It would provide the nation with an educated citizenry, so important in a democratic society. And they recognized that publicly supported education was essential to providing equality of opportunity for everyone, regardless of background or financial means. Strong beliefs about the importance of education are an integral part of the American Dream. We see it in such iconic visuals that are adorned in our minds, including a young Abe Lincoln reading by candlelight, Norman Rockwell's "Apple for the Teacher" cover on the *Saturday Evening Post*, or the classic line from the movie Dead Poet's Society, *Carpe diem.*

Appendices

Boston Latin School
Historic Milestones and Timeline
1635-2022

1635 On April 23, at a Boston town meeting, forty-five prominent colonists agree to fund the establishment of a Latin grammar school. Mr. Philemon Portmort is appointed Master. He begins conducting classes in his home.

1642 Harvard College publishes its first set of entrance requirements, which then set the standards for the early Latin School curriculum. A long-standing Latin School-Harvard relationship now begins.

1645 The first schoolhouse is erected on the north side of School Street. Occupied until 1704, it would later become the Head Master's residence.

1670 The first of the school's most Memorable Masters, Ezekiel Cheever is appointed. He will serve with distinction for thirty-eight years. A memorial tablet is mounted today on the wall of the corridor adjacent to the school's main entrance.

1674 Cotton Mather graduates from the Latin School, later becoming one of the most prominent colonial theologians and author of more than 350 published works.

1704 The second of the schoolhouses is now opened—a two-story, clapboard structure on the north side of School Street.

1708 Nathaniel Williams becomes Master, following the death of the memorable Ezekiel Cheever at age 94. Williams, the first former pupil to serve, would remain for 26 years.

1714 Benjamin Franklin enters the Latin School but leaves in less than two years. An eight-foot bronze statue of him is erected in 1865, overlooking the site of the first School Street building. It is one of the historic sites on the famous Boston Freedom Trail.

1735 Latin School celebrates its 100th birthday. John Lovell becomes Head Master, and serves for forty-one years, until the start of the Revolutionary War.

1748 The school moves into its third home, an all-brick structure on the south side of School Street. Enrollment now totals 120 students.

1773 Protests against British-imposed taxes on the colonists intensify, leading to the Boston Tea Party—a rebellious act instigated largely by BLS alumnus Samuel Adams.

1775 On April 18, Adams, along with fellow alumnus John Hancock, are in Lexington hiding from British troops. The soldiers march that night to Lexington in pursuit of them.

On the morning of April 19, the first shots of the Revolutionary War are fired on Lexington Green. That same day, Latin School Master John Lovell closes the school, announcing, "War's begun and school's done ... *deponite libros*," or, "*put away your books.*" Shortly thereafter, Lovell, a British loyalist, flees to Canada.

1776 On June 5, following the evacuation of Boston by the British, the school is reopened under a new Master, Samuel Hunt. He will hold that position for the next 29 years. On July 4, the Declaration in Independence is signed by five Latin School alumni: Benjamin Franklin, Samuel Adams, John Hancock, Robert Treat Paine, and William Hooper.

1791 The first of the Franklin medals are awarded. Franklin's legacy continues today, honoring the school's top scholars.

1798 Charles Bulfinch, BLS 1777, a noted architect, designs the still-standing Massachusetts State House on the crest of Beacon Hill. Later he is commissioned to supervise the rebuilding of the Capitol building in Washington.

1812 The school's fourth School Street building is erected. It is a three-story, granite-front structure, and would be the home of the school for the next 32 years.

1814 Benjamin Apthorp Gould becomes Master. He introduces declamation into the curriculum, as well as misdemeanor marks and report cards.

1837 Wendell Phillips, BLS 1827, joins with William Lloyd Garrison in the abolitionist movement and, as an orator, becomes its leading voice. On July 4, Ralph Waldo Emerson, BLS 1817, commemorates the Concord Minutemen battle of that day in 1775 with his famous poem, *The Concord Hymn*, and its famous line, "The shot heard round the world."

1844 The BLSA is formed as a volunteer alumni support organization, and the first of its kind for a public school.

1845 The school moves from School Street to a new Bedford Street location, its fifth. There are now an estimated 200 students.

1849 Charles William Eliot graduates from the school. He later becomes one of the nation's most respected educators. He serves as Harvard University president for 40 years.

1851 Francis Gardner, another of the school's most Memorable Masters, is appointed Head Master, the first to hold that title. He serves 25 years in that position. He was a Latin scholar but was best known as a stern disciplinarian.

1852 Curriculum changes are made, with the addition of English grammar and composition for Classes VI and IV. French is also added.

1856 Charles Sumner, BLS 1826, and a U.S. senator from Massachusetts, is attacked and badly beaten on the Senate floor, following his delivery of a fiery abolitionist speech.

1865 Henry Ward Beecher, BLS 1830, prominent clergyman and orator, is invited by Abraham Lincoln to speak at the Fort Sumter flag-raising, marking the end of the Civil War. Like fellow alumni abolitionists Phillips and Sumner, he had studied declamation at the Latin School.

1868 The Boston School Committee undertakes a review of the role of the Latin School and its classical curriculum in the city's education system. Counsel is sought from Head Master Gardner, as well as Charles William Eliot, now a nationally recognized educator.

1870 In December 1870, the statue of Alma Mater, commemorating those who served in the Civil War, is dedicated. It is the oldest Civil War commemorative sculpture, a representation of Minerva, with the names of fifty-one BLS alumni who died in the War engraved on her shield. The featured speaker at the dedication was United States Secretary of State and BLS alumnus William Maxwell Evarts. Placed originally at the entranceway of the then Bedford Street schoolhouse, it stands now in the main foyer of the Avenue Louis Pasteur building. The statue was the work of sculptor Richard Saltonstall Greenough, BLS 1829.

1876 After a series of interim changes are made in the curriculum, Eliot's recommendations for more balance between modern and classical studies are largely implemented. More emphasis is placed on English grammar and composition, the natural sciences, and the addition of German as a second foreign language. The new curriculum would essentially remain in place well into the twentieth century. Moses Merrill becomes Head Master upon the death of Francis Gardner. Like other memorable and long-serving Masters, his tenure would last for thirty-four years.

1877 A petition filed with the Boston School Committee to admit women is denied. A year later, the Girls Latin School is opened with thirty-seven pupils.

1880 The sixth, and then most elaborate home for the school, is opened on Warren Street. The three-story brick and stone structure have twenty-four classrooms, as well as a gym, science labs, and military drill hall. A similar opposite-side structure houses the English High School.

1881 The *Latin School Register* is founded as the first school magazine in the country. Its editor is George Santayana, BLS 1882, later a renowned philosopher, novelist, and essayist. On October 22, the Boston Symphony Orchestra gives its inaugural performance. The founder and its major patron is Henry Lee Higginson, BLS 1851, a Boston banker and philanthropist.

1884 John Fitzgerald, maternal grandfather of John F. Kennedy, graduates. Fitzgerald becomes the first Boston-born mayor of Irish descent.

1887 The first of the annual Thanksgiving Day football games between the Latin School and English High School is played at Harvard Stadium. It continues today as the oldest school sports rivalry in the country.

1890 A twenty-year wave of European immigration begins, with the sons of these immigrants soon to change the ethnic makeup of the Latin School.

1891 Students are offered a language curriculum choice between French and German.

1908 Joseph P. Kennedy, the father of President John F. Kennedy, graduates from the Latin School and later becomes a prominent banker and government official in the Franklin Roosevelt administration.

1913 Greek is no longer mandatory in the curriculum. It can be substituted by German.

1920 Patrick T. Campbell, reflecting the growing ethnic diversity of the faculty, becomes Head Master and the first of four others of Irish descent who would follow him. The school's enrollment now passes the 1,000-mark.

1922 The school moves into a newly constructed Avenue Louis Pasteur building in the Fenway. It will become the school's permanent home. The building quickly becomes overcrowded, forcing the construction of additional classrooms, and use of annex locations.

1929 Joseph Lawrence Powers becomes Head Master after 23 years at the school teaching mathematics. He will guide the school through the austerity years of the Great Depression and World War II, retiring in 1948.

1933 The school's building is renovated and doubled in size to accommodate a student body that has now reached 2,250. Chemistry is added to the curriculum.

1935 The school celebrates its 300th anniversary, with the ceremonies attended by the city's notables at Symphony Hall. Lee J. Dunn is the coordinating secretary. A Tercentenary tablet is created, and the school's history is published by the Harvard University Press.

1937 Wade H. McCree, Jr. graduates from the school. He becomes the first African American appointed to the U.S. Court of Appeals. He also served later as U.S. Solicitor General. In 1999, his name was added to the upper frieze of the Assembly Hall.

1941 U.S. enters World War II. After the war, a bronze tablet is mounted in the school entranceway, commemorating the ninety-eight alumni who died in the war.

1954 John Joseph Doyle becomes the school's Head Master. His career was to span 40 years in the Boston school system. Advance Placement courses are added during the Doyle tenure.

1957 Philip Marson, a 31-year Memorable Master in English, retires. In retirement, he writes three books on education and his Latin School experience.

1961 On January 20, John F. Kennedy, son of alumnus Joseph P. Kennedy, is inaugurated as the nation's thirty-fifth president. The Boston Latin School Band marches in the inaugural parade, representing the State of Massachusetts.

1962 Theodore H. White, BLS 1932, a political journalist, is awarded a Pulitzer Prize for his book *The Making of the President*, the story of the John F. Kennedy's presidential campaign of 1960.

1965 In December, beloved retired Master Max Levine dies after a 60-year association with the school as a student, highly revered head of the French Department, and active alumnus. The funeral eulogy is given by Rabbi Joseph Schubow, BLS 1916. Military drill and participation of the School Boy Parade is ended after 105 years.

1972 In September, girls are admitted to the school for the first time. Within a short time, they will represent more than half the student body.

1974 In June, a Federal Court under the jurisdiction of Judge W. Arthur Garrity issues a landmark Boston school desegregation order. It calls for cross-neighborhood busing of students to correct what were seen as imbalances in the racial makeup of the city's public schools.

1975 In September, the second part of the Garrity ruling takes effect, requiring the Latin School and two other city "exam" schools to accept 35 percent of its new students from Black and Hispanic applicants.

1977 Michael G. Contompasis is appointed Head Master and will lead the school through the challenging twenty-one-year affirmative action period. Later, active in Boston School Committee affairs, he becomes the city's Superintendent of Schools. Arthur Fiedler, a BLS alumnus and fifty-year conductor of the Boston Pops, is awarded the Presidential Medal of Freedom. He dies three years later.

1980 Leonard Bernstein, BLS 1935, noted composer and conductor, is awarded Kennedy Center Honors for "his lifetime contribution to American culture."

1985 The school celebrates its 350th anniversary. The keynote address is given by Clifton E. Wharton, Jr., a Black alumnus, Class of 1943, who had a long and distinguished career as an educator, philanthropist, foreign policy, and economic development executive.

1987 The BLSA launches the first of its Annual Fund drives.

1989 Renovations are completed of the school's Assembly Hall and cafeteria. A new gym and athletic facilities are also added.

1995 In spite of recent building renovations, a New England accrediting organization issues a warning to the school to upgrade its academic facilities, particularly citing the need for a new library.

1997 In September, the school ends the first phase of its affirmative action policies that had mandated admission of 35 percent Blacks and Hispanics. The action resulted from a pending suit involving the denial of admission to a white girl, whose admission test scores outperformed Black and Hispanics who were nonetheless given admission.

1998 In November, a three-judge panel strikes down the affirmative action admission plan that had temporarily replaced the original 35 percent mandate. The affirmative action era, which began in 1975, now comes to an end. Cornelia A. Kelley becomes the school's first female Head Master. She had been Chair of the Classics Department and Assistant Head Master for Administration.

2000 The BLSA launches the *Pons Privatus* campaign that raises $30 million for the school. It is the largest fundraising effort ever undertaken by a public school.

2002 A major three-year expansion and renovation of the school is completed. It includes a 12,500 square foot library, a new wing with two floors for art and music rooms, and a new dining hall.

2007 Lynne Mooney Teta is appointed Head Master, the second female to head the school. A 1986 graduate of the school, she had been an Assistant Head Master.

2009 Peter G. Kelly, BLS Class of 1983, is appointed president of the Boston Latin School Association.

2010 The school marks its 375th anniversary, with ceremonies held at Boston's historic King's Chapel. An address is given by Harvard University President, Drew Gilpen Faust, reaffirming the long-standing Latin School-Harvard relationship.

2012 The BLSA launches the *Prima Perpetua* campaign that raises $54,040,20—the largest fundraising effort ever undertaken by a public high school.

2017 Rachael Skerritt is appointed Head Master, becoming the first person of color to lead the Latin School. She is the first to be Head of School, as the title was changed during her tenure. Skerritt is a BLS alumna and previously worked as a teacher at the school, before moving up to the Boston Public Schools central office.

2022 Jason Gallagher is appointed Head of School.

Benjamin Franklin Thirteen Virtues

1. **TEMPERANCE:** Eat not to dullness; drink not to elevation.

2. **SILENCE:** Speak not but what may benefit others or yourself; avoid trifling conversation.

3. **ORDER:** Let all your things have their places; let each part of your business have its time.

4. **RESOLUTION:** Resolve to perform what you ought; perform without fail what you resolve.

5. **FRUGALITY:** Make no expense but to do good to others or yourself, i.e., waste nothing.

6. **INDUSTRY:** Lose no time; be always employed in something useful; cut off all unnecessary actions.

7. **SINCERITY:** Use no hurtful deceit; think innocently and justly, and, if you speak, speak accordingly.

8. **JUSTICE:** Wrong none by doing injuries or omitting the benefits that are your duty.

9. **MODERATION:** Avoid extremes; forbear resenting injuries so much as you think they deserve.

10. **CLEANLINESS:** Tolerate no uncleanness in body, clothes, or habitation.

11. **TRANQUILITY:** Be not disturbed at trifles, or at accidents common or unavoidable.

12. **CHASTITY:** Rarely use venery but for health or offspring, never to dullness, weakness, or the injury of your own or another's peace or reputation.

13. **HUMILITY:** Imitate Jesus and Socrates.

Source: The Library of Congress

Boston Latin School List of Head of Schools

Philemon Pormort	1635-1638
Daniel Maude	1638-1643
John Woodbridge	1643-1649
Robert Woodmancy	1649-1667
Benjamin Tompson	1667-1670
Ezekiel Cheever	1670-1708
Nathaniel Williams	1708-1734
John Lovell	1734-1775
Samuel Hunt	1776-1805
William Biglow	1805-1814
Benjamin Apthorp Gould	1814-1828
Frederic Percival Leverett	1828-1831
Charles Knapp Dillaway	1831-1836
Epes Sargent Dixwell	1836-1851
Francis Gardner	1851-1876
Augustine Milton Gay	1876
Moses Merrill	1876-1901
Arthur Irving Fiske	1902-1909
Henry Pennypacker	1910-1920
Patrick Thomas Campbell	1920-1929
Joseph Lawrence Powers	1929-1948
George Leonard McKim	1948-1954

John Joseph Doyle	1954-1964
Wilfred Leo O'Leary	1964-1976
Michael George Contompasis	1977-1998
Cornelia A. Kelley	1998-2007
Lynne Mooney Teta	2007-2016
Rachel Skerritt	2017-2022
Jason Gallagher	2022-

Prominent Latin School Alumni

(PARTIAL LIST)

John Leverett	Harvard College President
Cotton Mather	Theologian, Author
Benjamin Franklin	Signer, Declaration of Independence
Samuel Adams	Signer, Declaration of Independence
Samuel Langdon	Harvard College President
James Bowdoin	Massachusetts Governor
Robert Treat Paine	Signer, Declaration of Independence
James Lovell	Member of Continental Congress
John Hancock	Signer, Declaration of Independence
William Hooper	Signer, Declaration of Independence
Henry Knox	Revolutionary War General
Christopher Gore	U.S. Senator
Charles Bulfinch	Architect, Capitol Building
John Collins Warren	Massachusetts Medical Society President
Edward Everett	Harvard University President
Ralph Waldo Emerson	Philosopher, Poet
Samuel Francis Smith	Author of "America"
Charles Sumner	U.S. Senator
Robert Charles Winthrop	Speaker, U.S. House of Representatives
Wendell Phillips	Orator and Abolition Leader
John Lothrop Motley	U.S. Diplomat

John Bernard Fitzpatrick	Catholic Bishop
Henry Ward Beecher	Anti-Slavery Abolition Leader
William Maxwell Evarts	Secretary of State
Charles Devens	U.S. Attorney General
Edward Everett Hale	Theologian
Frances James Child	Author and Orator
Charles William Eliot	Harvard University President
Samuel Pierpont Langley	Aviation Pioneer
Phillip Brooks	Theologian
Henry Lee Higginson	Philanthropist
Martin Milmore	Sculptor
Matthew Harkins	Catholic Bishop
George Santayana	Philosopher
Joseph P. Kennedy	Government Official
Leonard Bernstein	Musical Conductor and Composer
Wade H. McCree	U.S. Solicitor General

Information and Data Sources

Boston Latin School Archives

Boston Public Library

Library of Congress

National Archives

Massachusetts Historical Society

The Boston Society

U.S. Census Bureau

U.S. Department of Homeland Security

U.S. Department of Education

National Education Association (NEA)

Massachusetts Department of Elementary and Secondary Education

Massachusetts Archives Collection

Boston School Committee

Boston Magazine

Harvard University Gazette

The Harvard Crimson

The Boston Globe

The New York Times

Washington University Law Review

Suffolk University Library Archives

Pew Research Center

Stanford Encyclopedia of Philosophy

Bibliography

BOSTON LATIN SCHOOL

Dunn, Lee J. (ed.). *Proceedings and Addresses of the Boston Latin School Tercentenary*. Boston Latin School Associates, Boston, 1937.

Holmes, Pauline. *A Tercentenary History of The Boston Public Latin School, 1635–1935*. Harvard University Press, Cambridge MA, 1935.

Jenks, Henry F. *Catalogue of The Boston Public Latin School Association established 1635 with a Historical Sketch*. Boston Latin School Associates, Boston MA, 1886.

Marson, Phillip. *A Teacher Speaks*. David McKay Company, New York, 1960.

Marson, Phillip. *Breeder of Democracy*. Schenkman Publishing Company, Cambridge, MA, 1963.

Marson, Phillip. *Yankee Voices*. Schenkman Publishing Company, Cambridge MA, 1967.

GENERAL REFERENCE

Bowman, John S. (ed.). *The Cambridge Dictionary of American Biography*. Cambridge University Press, New York, 1995.

Fornier, Eric and Garraty, John A. *Readers Companion to American History*. Houghton Mifflin Company, New York, 1993.

Morison, Samuel Eliot. *The Oxford History of the American People: Vol I, Prehistory to 1789*. Penguin Books, New York, 1994.

Morison, Samuel Eliot. *The Oxford History of the American People: Vol. II, 1789 Through Reconstruction*. Penguin Books, New York, 1994.

Morison, Samuel Eliot. *The Oxford History of the American People: Vol. III: 1869-1963*. Penguin Books, New York, 1994.

O'Connor, Thomas H. *Boston A to Z*. Harvard University Press, Cambridge, MA, 2000.

HISTORY & SOCIAL SCIENCE

Adams, James Truswell. *The Epic of America*. Simon Publications, 2001.

Barkan, Elliott Robert (ed.). *A Nation of Peoples: A Sourcebook on America's Multicultural Heritage*. Greenwood Press, Westport, CT, 1999.

Boorstin, Daniel J. *The Americans: The Colonial Experience*. Random House, New York, 1958.

Brooks, Van Wyck. *The Flowering of New England: 1815-1865*. Ameron Ltd., 1981.

Cammisa, James V. Jr. *The American Dream: How the Free-Market Economy Is Eroding It and What We Can Do to Restore It*. Kindle Direct Publishing, Seattle, WA, 2012.

Clarke, Ted. *Beacon Hill, Back Bay, and the Building of Boston's Golden Age*. The History Press, Charleston, SC, 2010.

Commager, Henry Steele. *The American Mind*. Yale University Press, New Haven, CT, 1950.

Cullen, Jim. *The American Dream: The History of an Idea that Shapes the Nation*. Oxford University Press, New York, 2003.

Daniels, Roger. *Coming to America: A History of Immigration and Ethnicity in American Life*. Harper Perennial, New York, 1991.

Emerson, Ralph Waldo. *Essays*. Gramercy Books, New York, 1993.

Fischer, David Hackett. *Paul Revere's Ride*. Oxford University Press, New York, 1994.

Franklin, Benjamin. *Poor Richard's Almanac*. Skyhorse Publishing, New York, 2007.

Handlin, Oscar. *Boston's Immigrants: 1790-1880*. Harvard University Press, Cambridge MA, 1991.

Harrison, Lawrence E. and Huntington, Samuel P. *Culture Matters: How Values Share Human Progress.* Basic Books, New York, 2008.

Highet, Gilbert. *The Classical Traditions: Greek and Roman Influences on Western Literature.* Oxford University Press, New York, 1985.

Jones, Howard Mumfard and Bessie Zaban (eds.). *The Many Voices of Boston: A Historical Anthology, 1630-1975.* Little Brown and Company, Boston, 1975.

Lipset, Seymour. *American Exceptionalism.* Norton, New York, 1996.

Lounsbury, Thomas R. (ed.). *Yale Book of American Verse.* Yale University Press, New Haven, CT, 1912.

Lowance, Mason (ed.). *Against Slavery; An Abolitionist Reader.* Penguin Books, New York, 2000.

Morison, Samuel Eliot. *Three Centuries of Harvard: 1636–1696.* Cambridge, MA, Harvard University Press, 1986.

O'Connor, Thomas H. *The Boston Irish: A Political History.* Back Bay Books, Boston, 1995.

Puleo, Stephen. *A City So Grand: The Rise of an American Metropolis, Boston 1850-1900.* Beacon Press, Boston, 2010

Schlesinger, Arthur M., Jr. *The Age of Jackson.* Little Brown, New York, 1945.

Tocqueville, Alexis N. *Democracy in America.* Perennial Modern Classics, New York, 2006.

Veda, Reed and Wright, Conrad E. (eds.). *Faces of Community: Immigrant Massachusetts 1860-2000.* Northeastern University Press, 2003.

Weber, Max. *The Protestant Ethic and the Spirit of Capitalism.* Charles Scribner's Sons, New York, 1953.

AUTOBIOGRAPHY/BIOGRAPHY

Applegate, Debby. *The Most Famous Man in America: A Biography of Henry Ward Beecher.* Doubleday, New York, 2006.

Bremer, Francis J. *John Winthrop: America's Forgotten Founding Father.* Oxford University Press, New York, 2003.

Donald, David. *Charles Sumner and the Coming of the Civil War.* Alfred A. Knopf, New York, 1960.

Goodwin, Doris Kearns. *The Fitzgeralds and the Kennedys: An American Saga.* Simon & Schuster, New York, 2001.

Hawkins, Hugh. *Between Harvard and America: The Educational Leadership of Charles W. Eliot.* Oxford University Press, New York, 1972.

Isaacson, Walter. *Benjamin Franklin: An American Life.* Simon & Schuster Paperbacks, New York, 2003.

Morgan, Edmund S. *The Puritan Dilemma: The Story of John Winthrop.* Longman, New York, 2006.

Redsone, Sumner. *A Passion to Win.* Simon & Schuster, New York, 2010

Silverman, Kenneth. *The Life and Times of Cotton Mather.* Harper & Rowe Publishers, New York, 1984.

Steward, James Brewer. *Wendell Phillips: Liberty's Here.* Louisiana State University Press. Baton Rouge, LA, 1986.

Stoll, Ira. *Samuel Adams—A Life.* Free Press, New York, 2002.

Unger, Harlow Giles. *John Hancock: Merchant King and American Patriot.* John Wiley & Sons, Inc. New York, 2000.

Zibb, Lazar. *The Career of John Cotton: Puritans and the American Experience.* Princeton University Press, Princeton, NJ, 1962.

EDUCATION

Kopff, E. Christian. *The Devil Knows Latin: Why America Needs the Classical Tradition.* Intercollegiate Studies Institute, 2001.

Dewey, John. *Democracy and Education.* NuVision Publishers, Sioux Falls, SD, 2009.

Finn, Chester E. and Hockett, Jessica A. *Exam Schools: Inside America's Most Selective Public High Schools*. Princeton University Press, Princeton, NJ, 2012.

Fuhrman, Susan and Lazerson, Maribel (eds.). *The Public Schools*. Oxford University Press, New York, 2005.

Goldin, Claudia and Katz, Lawrence F. *The Race Between Education and Technology*. The Belknap Press, Cambridge, MA, 2008.

Kaestle, Carl F. *Pillars of the Republic: Common Schools and American Society, 1780-1860*. Hill and Wang, New York, 1983.

LaVague-Manty, Mika. *The Playing Fields of Eton*. University of Michigan Press, Ann Arbor, MI, 2009.

Likena, Thomas. *Educating for Character*. Bantam Books, New York 1991.

Murphy, Madonna M. *Character Education in America's Blue Ribbon Schools*. Technomic Publishing Co., Lancaster, PA, 1998.

Perrin, Christopher A. *An Introduction to Classical Education*. Classical Academic Press, Camp Hill, PA, 2004.

Ravitch, Diane. *Left Back: A Century of Failed School Reforms*. Simon & Schuster, New York, 2000.

Ravitch, Diane and Vinovskis, Marsis. *Learning From the Past: What History Tells Us About School Reform*. John Hopkins University Press, Baltimore, 1995.

Reese, William J. *The Origins of the American High School*. Yale University Press, New Haven, CT, 1995.

Ryan, Kevin and Bohlin, Karen E. *Building Character Schools*. Jossey Bass, San Francisco, 1999.